Advocating for the Child in Protection Proceedings

A Handbook for Lawyers and Court Appointed Special Advocates

Donald N. Duquette
University of Michigan Law School

with

Martha W. Steketee
David Murphey
Karin Elliott
Liese A. Hull
Roger Lauer

Lisa D'Aunno
Meryl Berlin
Sandra Bermann
Andrea Hansell
David Rowe

Lexington Books
D.C. Heath and Company/Lexington, Massachusetts/Toronto

Support for this book was provided in part by the Bush Program in Child
Development and Social Policy of the University of Michigan, supported by
the Bush Foundation of St. Paul, Minnesota, and by the Cook Research
Fund of the University of Michigan Law School. The Proposal for
Legislation Establishing a Statewide Child Advocacy Office and Setting
Standards for Representing the Child (appendix A) was developed with help
from the National Center on Child Abuse and Neglect, which provides the
University of Michigan and nine other universities with funds for
interdisciplinary training programs in child abuse and neglect.

Duquette, Donald N.
    Advocating for the child in protection proceedings : a handbook for
lawyers and court appointed special advocates / Donald N. Duquette with
Martha W. Steketee. . . [et all.].
       p.   cm.
   ISBN 0-669-21465-5 (alk. paper)
    1. Children—Legal status, laws, etc.—Michigan. 2. Child abuse-
Law and legislation—Michigan. 3. Custody of children—
Michigan. 4. Legal assistance to children—Michigan. I. Steketee,
Martha W. II. Title.
KFM4550.C4D86   1990
344.774'03276—dc20
[347.74043276]

Published simultaneously in Canada
Printed in the United States of America
Casebound International Standard Book Number: 0-669-21465-5
Library of Congress Catalog Card Number: 89-13455

The paper used in this publication meets the minimum requirements of
American National Standard for Information Sciences—Permanence of
Paper for Printed Library Materials, ANSI Z39.48-1984. ∞ ™

Year and number of this printing:

92 10 9 8 7 6 5 4 3 2

*To my beloved wife, Kathy Duquette, and to Gail, our daughter.
May all children be loved as Gail is.*

Contents

Preface

The Child Advocacy Law Clinic at University of Michigan Law School has represented children in child abuse and neglect cases since 1976 in several Michigan countries. I hope that this book helps others—lawyers and nonlawyers alike—take advantage of our experience and become even more effective as champions for children alleged to be abused or neglected by their parents or caretakers.

Throughout the United States, lawyers are typically appointed to represent children in these cases, presumably because the child advocate is expected to speak up in court in behalf of the child. I have often wondered, however, whether a traditionally trained lawyer acting alone with no special training is the best voice for the child in these proceedings. Much of the skill and background required to be a good child advocate comes from psychology and social work. The tenacity and commitment required knows no disciplinary bounds. Legal skills are important, of course, but not sufficient in and of themselves. Either the lawyer should receive special training in child advocacy or ought to work with a person who has.

In fall 1987 the University of Michigan Bush Program in Child Development and Public Policy sponsored a Child Advocacy Work Group composed of graduate fellows from law, social work, political science, and psychology. The Group provided the opportunity to explore questions about representing children: Who ought to represent the child? What ought to be the training of this advocate, and what ought to be the duties? For two years Bush fellows reviewed the literature, represented children in child protection proceedings, and reflected upon those experiences. Their experiences and reflections were assembled into a work product that forms the basis of this book.

We have tried to keep the book short, practical, and straightforward, though the articulation of the child advocate role presented here speaks to a serious debate in the academic literature and has significant public policy implications. We have four audiences in mind. First and foremost we hope that court appointed special advocates (CASAs) find this work practically useful as they assume the important task of speaking up for a child. CASAs are typically nonlawyer volunteers appointed by the court to represent the child. The CASA movement is growing rapidly in the United States, but the role is not clearly articulated nor is there a consensus about what CASAs are to do. They need guidance and training. We hope this book helps.

Second, we hope that lawyers seeking to represent the child more effectively will find the book useful because of the way it breaks down the advocate role and fits it into the traditional legal context. Lawyers looking for practical guidance in a role that requires skills from several disciplines—law, psychology, and social work—will find assistance here, as will lawyers asked to work closely with lay volunteers acting as CASAs or guardians ad litem.

Third, policymakers and community leaders such as judges, agency directors, and existing child advocates, who are trying to understand the role of the child advocate and make that role more effective, should get ideas for organizing and supervising a program in their jurisdictions.

Finally, teachers of social work, psychology, and law may find this book of assistance in teaching courses in child welfare and child advocacy. We hope that academics in all of these disciplines find our articulation of the role of the child advocate of considerable interest.

We owe a debt of gratitude to Harold Stevenson, professor of psychology and director of the Bush Program at the University of Michigan. He invited development of the Child Advocacy Work Group, supported us throughout, and encouraged publication of our manuscript. Lisa D'Aunno, my law school collegue in the Child Advocacy Law Clinic, was herself a Bush fellow as a law student—the first Michigan law student to do so—and served as coleader in the first year of the work group. She provided valuable comments on the early drafts and encouragement throughout.

Judge Thomas Gadola of the Genesee County Probate Court, a child advocate and a staunch supporter of the University of Michigan, allowed fellows from our work group to represent children in his court under lawyer supervision. Our work could not have been completed but for his support and the support of his excellent court staff.

Clinical teaching at an institution like the University of Michigan brings many rewards, but chief among them is the satisfaction of working with graduate and professional students of such high caliber. The nine Bush fellows who participated in the development of this book were carefully screened for their ability and commitment, and it was a delight to work with each of them. The words of fellows who participated in the second year appear here more often than the words of the first-year fellows. The second year stood on the shoulders of the first year, however, and learned much from their notes and conversations.

Among the fellows, Martha Steketee deserves special mention. Martha was the only fellow to participate in the Child Advocacy Work Group for two years and, in addition to doing her share of the drafting, assumed special responsibility for organizing and producing our early work product. I called on her many times in the final drafting and editing of this book for her advice and assistance.

All who participated in developing this book hope that other child advocates—both lay volunteers and lawyers—find our observations useful. Most important, we sincerely hope that our efforts here help other advocates achieve that ever-elusive goal: the best interests of their client, the child.

I
The Context of Child Advocacy

1

Introduction

Most people first appointed to represent a child feel intimidated, unsure, insecure, and somewhat awed by the responsibility: "How can I add anything to a case plan for a child that a professional social worker has developed? How can I presume to tell the experienced and powerful judge anything he or she has not already thought of herself? How can I care more for this child than his or her parents, grandparents, or other extended family members? How can I presume to identify the 'best interests of the child', much less achieve that lofty goal?" Nonlawyers will wonder, in addition, how they can stand up to lawyers who are professionally trained in advocacy.

In fact, the independent advocate for the child can be influential and important in child protection proceedings. Unlike the other participants in this drama, the advocate has no other interest but that of the child. The court, in contrast, must balance the rights of the parents, the state, and the child. The social agencies have limited resources, which they have to spread over far too many children. The lawyers represent specific interests of the parents, and agency, or other litigants. Although most of these other participants state their goals in terms of the child's interests and may sincerely try to achieve the child's interests, the child advocate is generally supreme in having only the interests of the child in mind.

The new advocate might still be concerned: "So what if my motives are pure and sincere; I don't have legions of social workers or counselors at my command. I don't have a graduate degree in social work or psychology. I don't have the power and prestige of the court. What can I do to help the child? I am only a lay volunteer willing to represent one or two children at a time." (Or, "I am only one lawyer fairly new at this.")

In fact, child advocates can accomplish a great deal for the child, as recent research has confirmed. The role of advocate is different and distinct from all others—the social worker, the case aide, the lawyers for parents or agency, or the parents—in the process.

The purpose of this book is to help child advocates become as good an advocate for individual children as possible. In the following pages, we will place the child advocate in a legal and social context of many agencies and several courts. We will describe how the role of the advocate has evolved over the years and is still not settled. We will explore the five roles of the child advocate:—fact finder, legal representative, case monitor, information and resource broker, and mediator-conciliator—and provide guidance for fulfilling those roles. Finally, we will take the advocate step by step through the legal process, applying the ten dimensions of child advocacy to each procedural stage of the legal child protection process using a case example.

The child advocate is not alone in this drama but is one of many players. The advocate's job is not personally to protect the child from harm but to see to it that the child is protected. The job is not to provide a permanent stable home for the child but to see that one is provided. The job is not to assess the family problems and strengths but to see that a thorough assessment is made. As one advocate put it, "It is not up to me to *be* the support system for the child but to ensure that a support system is in place."

Child advocates may work as a team. Commonly CASA programs provide consultation and support to the individual advocates. Two CASAs may work together, or a lawyer and a CASA may team up on behalf of a child. The value of a supportive group in advocacy work can hardly be overstated.

The child advocate role presented here is broad and ambitious. The advocate plays on a large field on behalf of his or her young client. There is an outmoded view of the advocate role in which the advocate's actions are circumscribed by the beginning and end of a particular court hearing. In contrast, we take a broad and long view of the child advocate role, beginning with appointment to act as an advocate in a particular child protection case. The child's interests are certainly affected by the child protection agency, the mother, the father, and the other litigants likely to appear in juvenile or family court, but other formal and informal institutions may affect the child considerably, for good or ill. Is extended family available as a resource or another source of danger? What social services can be marshaled for the child? Can the school assist? Are there recreational programs such as scouting, sports, and camps that may help the youngster (and, perhaps, the parents)? Are other courts involved in the youngster's life? For example, the child may be involved in a custody case in the divorce court; in this case, the divorce court could provide the necessary legal protection for the child. In cases of sexual abuse or serious physical abuse, the criminal courts may be involved. Can the advocate assist the child in those procedures? How do other court actions affect the civil child protection proceedings?

The child advocate can play an important integration and coordination role in responding to the needs of a child. When so many people and so many institutions are involved on behalf of a child, sometimes responsibility gets lost, and no one seems to be in charge. The child advocate can be the thread that pulls many of these resources and caring people together to present the court a meaningful plan for the child.

No single book can satisfy all the needs of the child advocate in every case in every community. Advocates are constantly researching issues and questions relevant to their children. The knowledge, information, and skills necessary to be a good child advocate require more than is presented here. This book is designed to be used by the child advocate as one resource among many others. Our focus is on the process and goals of advocacy. We have attempted to create a framework for advocacy that will help organize the advocate's efforts. We make several assumptions as to other training and background information the advocate needs.

1. Child development. We assume that advocates have some basic knowledge of child development—the abilities and the needs of children at various ages—and that advocates understand the "child's sense of time" and the need for permanence and stability in a child's life. The advocate needs to understand the concept of permanency planning and the practices that promote permanency for children.

2. Local court procedures. Although we describe typical court procedure and the common elements of state law, each jurisdiction has its own variations. Child advocates should understand local court procedures and practices. For advocates who are not lawyers, legal consultation should be continuously available.

3. Children's service agencies. The structure, organization, and key personnel of local social services and agencies vary from community to community. It is extremely important for the advocate to understand this structure, know the individuals involved, and, especially, understand the operation of child protective services and foster care.

4. Other social services. Advocates should know which other social services in the locale are available for children and their families (among them services for substance abuse, child sexual abuse, counseling, and public health services), and they should know the principal staff persons. Some jurisdictions provide a written summary of the most commonly available services with names and telephone numbers of the contact persons.

5. Privacy and preference for family. We assume that advocates understand the tension between privacy and state intervention. Advocates should understand and appreciate the legal rights of parents and children to be left alone, free of government interferences, and the traditional American values that underlie that philosophy. The public policy of the states has been to prefer the natural family of the child over other long-term placement. Reasonable efforts should be made to protect the child in the biological home and to rehabilitate natural parents so they can provide adequately for the child, as long as the child is safe and rehabilitation of the biological family can be done in a reasonable time considering the age of the child. Only when parents have been given an opportunity to make their home safe for the child and have failed to correct problems or where no rehabilitation measures are likely to be successful should aggressive steps be taken

to find an alternative permanent plan for the child, possibly through termination of parental rights and adoption.

6. Definition of child abuse and neglect. Although we touch on the concept of child abuse and neglect, we assume that the definition of child abuse and neglect is explored more fully as part of the training and preparation of the advocate and in the context of the advocate's particular jurisdiction. The advocate should appreciate the cultural relativity and subjectivity of the concept of child maltreatment (discussed in chapter 4). After reviewing state statutes, case law, and current practices of the local courts, advocates should understand the standard of child abuse, neglect, and maltreatment used in their community. The juvenile or family court judge is particularly suited to assist in clarifying local community standards in this regard.

Although the challenges and frustrations may be many, there are few other roles as satisfying as speaking up for a child.

2
History and Legal Context

Common Law Roots

Only in fairly recent history have courts routinely appointed an independent representative for the child as part of child protection proceedings when abuse or neglect is alleged. As is the case with so much of the rest of U.S. law and legal traditions, the role of the independent advocate traces its origins to the common law of England where the king assumed responsibility for protecting persons, such as children and the mentally ill, who were unable to protect themselves.[1] When a child needed protection in court, the king would issue a letter patent for the appointment of a guardian to represent the child's interests. In the United States a guardian ad litem was appointed for the child when the child was involved in a lawsuit. *Black's Law Dictionary* defines guardian ad litem as "a special guardian appointed by the court to prosecute or defend, in behalf of an infant or incompetent, a suit to which he is a party, and such guardian is considered an officer of the court to represent the interest of the infant or incompetent in the litigation."[2] State laws currently permit or require a court to appoint a guardian ad litem for the child who has a potential interest in money or property that is the subject of litigation.[3] In order for a child to sue someone to enforce the child's legal rights, an adult must act as "next friend" on behalf of the child. A child who is a defendant in a suit would be represented by a guardian ad litem. Today, however, the terms *next friend* and *guardian ad litem* are used almost interchangeably.[4] Thus, in court actions where money or property is at stake, the court takes special precautions on behalf of the child.

The name *guardian ad litem* has been applied widely in most jurisdictions to identify the independent advocate for the child in child protection proceedings. This imprecise use of the term *"guardian ad litem"* fails to reflect the fact that the responsibilities of the advocate in protection proceedings are somewhat different from what they are for the guardian ad litem in civil litigation. In addition, in child protection cases, the interests of the child are ordinarily psychological rather than monetary.

The Independent Advocate

Other Legal Settings

From the same common law roots, the practice of appointing a representative of the child in a variety of legal settings has evolved. Children have substantial interests at stake in child custody disputes surrounding divorce or in disputed guardianship proceedings. Many states' statutes authorize the courts to appoint special legal representation for the child in custody proceedings.[5] A local child advocacy office may be ideally suited to offer representation in these cases.[6]

Similarly children who are involved in the criminal justice system as victims or witnesses, or both, often need an advocate to guide them through the process. Debra Whitcomb has identified several potential functions of a guardian ad litem for the child in criminal court:[7] to act as counselor and interpreter of the legal process for the youngster; to protect the child against system-related trauma; to serve as a linchpin connecting several agencies and courts; to provide a voice for the child through a victim impact statement, at bail hearings, or sentencing, for example; or to serve as an advocate for the child's legal rights.[7] Several states have enacted legislation authorizing appointment of a guardian ad litem for the child in criminal proceedings.[8] A local child advocacy office established primarily to serve children in protection cases may also be well suited to represent children in the criminal justice process. The responsibilities are great, however, and the setting is quite different from the juvenile or family court. A program established to represent children in civil protection proceedings should proceed with caution and not overextend itself.

Whether the office is appointed by a court to represent the child officially in the criminal justice system or in a child custody dispute, the advocate for the child in the civil child protection proceedings should be aware of any other legal proceedings that may affect the child or the outcome of the child protection case. Although the advocate may not have official standing in the other proceedings without an order from the court, he or she can usually keep track of and follow these other matters and can attempt to coordinate decisions between and among the various courts and attorneys. Unfortunately children regularly get caught up in a net of various legal actions where no single person acts to coordinate among them. An advocate for a child in the civil child protection case should make it his or her business to find out what is happening and communicate that to the attorneys and the courts so that any negative impact on the child is lessened.

Child Protection Cases

The focus of this book is independent representation of the child in civil child protection cases. Based on the same common law roots already discussed, individual judges and state legislatures recognized the need and began appointing independent child advocates. The practice became increasingly accepted. In 1962 the New York legislature created a system of "law guardians" to provide legal representation for minors in neglect and juvenile delinquency cases.[9] Colorado was the first state to require appointment of a guardian in child abuse cases.[10] Other states began passing similar legislation either permitting or requiring appointment of an independent advocate for the child.

In 1974 the U.S. Congress enacted the Child Abuse and Neglect Prevention and Treatment Act, which required, as a condition of states' receiving federal funds, the appointment of a guardian ad litem to represent the child in child abuse or neglect cases that resulted in a judicial proceeding.[11] The guardian ad litem did not have to be an attorney, and the regulations implementing the act specified few duties.[12] In the 1988 reauthorization of the act, Congress continues to require appointment of a guardian ad litem to represent the child in child protection proceedings but is silent on the representative's duties.[13] The 1988 act also requires the federal government to evaluate the effectiveness of independent child representatives in each state "through the use of guardian ad litem and court appointed special advocates" and to recommend how to improve legal representation of children in cases of child abuse or neglect.[14]

Determining the Child's Representative and Role

There is now a general agreement in the United States that the child ought to be independently represented. The debate has now moved to questions of how the child ought to be represented and by whom and what the proper training ought to be. Although state laws in nearly every U.S. jurisdiction require that children be independently represented in civil child protection proceedings, there is no clear description and definition of the role and duties of an independent child advocate.[15] Lawyers provide the vast majority of representation for children in these cases. Nonetheless, many are dissatisfied with the quality of representation children receive in these proceedings and complain about a lack of direction as to what they should actually do in fulfillment of the child advocate role. Lawyers ordinarily receive no special training in representing children in child abuse and neglect cases and often feel the need for it.

In 1978 Donald Bross from the Kempe Center for the Prevention of Child Abuse and Neglect in Denver, Colorado, and others organized the National Association of Counsel for Children (NACC). Originally the organization was open primarily to lawyers and was intended to provide training and information to child advocates. Now the NACC membership includes professionals from law, medicine, social work, mental health, and law enforcement. It has over 600 members in forty-seven states and nine countries working on behalf of children affected by legal proceedings. The organization sponsors conferences, publishes books and a newsletter, supports amicus curiae positions on important court cases affecting children, and acts as a resource for practitioners and the general public who need information and referrals.[16]

The question of whether someone other than a lawyer can represent children in these proceedings has been raised in several quarters. The American Bar Association's Juvenile Justice Standards Project noted in 1980 that a representative trained wholly in the law may not be the appropriate choice for representing children in protective proceedings:

> It would not seem irresponsible to suggest that a professional trained in psychology, psychiatry, social psychology, or social welfare be assigned the initial responsibility for protecting children under these circumstances. There is, however, no evidence that this alternative is presently available, either in terms of numbers of competent personnel or in terms of occupational independence from official and interested agencies. . . .
>
> Until there are sufficient numbers of independent, competent personnel trained in other disciplines who will undertake to ascertain and guard the child's interests in these proceedings, continued reliance on legal representation for the child is necessary.[17]

Efforts are under way to develop competent personnel, independent of courts and agencies, to fulfill the child advocacy function. We may be nearing the day when advocates other than lawyers, but working with lawyer consultation, may be able to represent children on a widespread basis.

The CASA Movement

The search for clarification of the advocate's role and for alternative ways to achieve effective representation for children has taken many forms. Communities throughout the nation have experimented with trained volunteers to represent the child or to assist a lawyer in representation of the child. In 1977, Seattle, Washington, began its guardian ad litem program using the name CASA (Court Appointed Special Advocates) to designate lay volunteers who represent children in child protection cases.[18] The Seattle CASAs worked under the supervision of a social worker and a lawyer and were viewed by themselves and the court as a substitute for court-appointed lawyers for children.[19] In the same year Judge Lindsay G. Arthur began an identical program in Minneapolis, Minnesota.[20] Since then the National Council of Family and Juvenile Court Judges has encouraged CASA development in many ways, including sponsoring national CASA seminars and programs.[21] The National Council of Jewish Women, after adopting CASA's as a special community service project, developed a manual for CASA programs and sponsored programs around the country.[22] The Junior League has been an important supporter of CASA programs in many cities.[23]

Perhaps the most notable national development has been the organization in 1982 of the National Court Appointed Special Advocate Association, which claims well over 200 local chapters from nearly every state. The CASAs are volunteer laypersons (nonlawyers) who are appointed by the juvenile or family court to act as representatives of the children. Several states have enacted statutes that expressly authorize CASA representation in child protection proceedings.[24] Research is showing that trained lay advocates with proper supervision can perform as well as or better than attorneys.[25] A recent national evaluation by the U.S. Department of Health and Human Services shows that the most common form of providing representation for children, by private attorneys with no special training, is the least effective of the five models they studied. In their estimation, two models in which CASAs participated were the most effective.[26]

The role of the CASA and other lay volunteer child advocates varies greatly from community to community. The volunteers may be paired with an attorney and become the "eyes and ears" of the child's lawyer, or the volunteer may be independent of the child's legal representative, doing separate investigations and independent advocacy for the child. Still other volunteer advocates function as assistants or adjuncts to the caseworkers.

There is a need to clarify the role of the independent child advocate, and that is one of the goals of this book. We reject a role in which the advocate acts as an aide to the caseworker or to the attorney. Instead we urge an aggressive role for the advocate as an equal member of a lawyer-lay advocate team.

Conclusion

The role of the independent advocate for the child has evolved from the common law and legislative initiative over the past two decades. As society has gained experience, new questions have arisen as to how the child ought to be represented, by whom, and what the proper training of the advocate ought to be. Innovations are occurring throughout the country in this regard. Although we must keep in mind that this advocacy occurs as part of a legal proceeding, there may be a significant place for trained and supervised nonlawyer advocates.

Notes

1. B. Fraser, "Independent Representation for the Abused and Neglected Child: The Guardian Ad Litem," *California Western Law Review* 13 (1976–1977): 28.

2. *Black's Law Dictionary*, 5th ed. (St. Paul, Minn.: 1979), p. 635

3. Most states model their applicable rule after the Federal Rules of Civil Procedure Rule 17 (c): "Whenever an infant has a representative, such as a general guardian, committee, conservator, or other like fiduciary the representative may sue or defend on

behalf of the infant. . . . If an infant . . . does not have a duly appointed representative he may sue by his next friend or by a guardian ad litem. The court shall appoint a guardian ad litem for an infant . . . not otherwise represented in action or shall make such other order as it deems proper for the protection of the infant." R. Horowitz and H. Davidson, *Legal Rights of Children*, (Colorado Springs, Col.: Shepards/McGraw Hill, 1984), §3.03

4. *American Jursiprudence, Second Edition*, (Rochester, N.Y.: The Lawyer's Cooperative Publishing Co., 1981) Infants §158.

5. Horowitz and Davidson, *Legal Rights,* §6.09.

6. However, A. Freud, J. Goldstein, and A.J. Solnit in their influential work, *Before the Best Interests of the Child* (New York: Free Press, 1979), discourage appointment of an independent advocate for the child in custody disputes. In the interests of being less intrusive into family privacy, they recommend that a child be independently represented only if the parent so requests or if emergency out-of-home placement or formal court jurisdiction displaces the parent as the primary representative of the child's interests.

7. D. Whitcomb, *Guardian Ad Litem in Criminal Courts*, (Washington, D.C.: U.S. Department of Justice, National Institute of Justice, February 1988).

8. Florida, Florida Statutes Annotated §914.17; Oklahoma, Oklahoma Statutes Annotated Tit. 21 846(B) (1985 Supp.); Iowa, Iowa Code Annotated §910A.15; New Hampshire, Superior Court Rule 93-A.

9. N.Y. Family Court Act §241-249a (McKinney 1975 & Supp.).

10. Note, "The Non-Lawyer Guardian ad Litem in Child Abuse and Neglect Proceedings: The King County, Washington Experience," *Washington Law Review* 58 (1983): 853, 854.

11. 42 United States Code §5103(b)(2)(G)(1976).

12. The regulations provide that the "guardian at litem need not be an attorney; however, such representative may be an attorney charged with presentation in a judicial proceeding of the evidence alleged to amount to the abuse and neglect, so long as his legal responsibility includes representing the rights, interests, welfare, and well-being of the child." 45 Cod of Federal Regulations §1340.3(d)(7) (1981).

13. Child Abuse Prevention, Adoption, and Family Services Act of 1988, Public Law (PL) 100-294, §8, 42 USC 5106a.

14. P.L. 1988 100-294, §104, 42 USC 5105.

15. See, for example, New York Family Court Act, §241-249a (McKinney); Michigan, Michigan Compiled Laws Annotated 722.630; Colorado, Colorado Revised Statutes 19-10-113; California, Calif. West's Ann. Cal. Welf. and Inst. Code §326; Texas, Uniform Texas Code Annotated Family Code §11.10; Florida, Florida Statutes Annotated 415.508.

16. National Association of Counsel for Children, *Representing Children: Current Issues in Law Medicine, Mental Health and Protective Services* (Denver: The Association, 1987). For more information, contact National Association of Counsel for Children, 1205 Oneida Street, Denver, Colorado 80220; (303) 321-3963.

17. American Bar Association, Institute of Judicial Administration, Juvenile Justice Standards Project, *Standards Relating to Counsel for Private Parties* (Cambridge, Mass.: Ballinger, 1980), pp. 73–74.

18. C. Ray-Bettineski, "Court Appointed Special Advocates: The Guardian ad Litem for Abused and Neglected Children," *Juvenile and Family Court Journal* (August, 1978): 65.

19. "Non-Lawyer Guardian," p. 862, n.65.

20. National Court Appointed Special Advocate Association, *Court Appointed Special Advocate—A Guide for Your Court* (Seattle, Wash. The Association 1988).

21. For information on programs, contact the Court Appointed Special Advocate Committee, National Council of Family and Juvenile Court Judges, Judicial College Building, University of Nevada, Reno, Nevada 89507.

22. M. Blady, *Children at Risk: Making a Difference through the Court Appointed Special Advocate Project* (1982) (available from the National Council of Jewish Women, 15 East 26th Street, New York, New York 10010).

23. See *A Guide for Your Court*.

24. North Carolina, North Carolina General Statutes sec. 7A-489, South Carolina, Children's Code §20-7-121; Texas, Uniform Texas Code Annotated, Family Code §11.101; California, West's Ann. Cal. Welf. and Inst. Code §356.5.

25. D.N. Duquette and S.H. Ramsey, "Representation of Children in Child Abuse and Neglect Cases: An Empirical Look at What Constitutes Effective Representation," *University of Michigan Journal of Law Reform 20* (1987): 341; Duquette and Ramsey, "Using Lay Volunteers to Represent Children in Child Protection Court Proceedings," *Child Abuse and Neglect: The International Journal* 10 (1986): 293–308; Department of Health and Human Services (HHS), *National Evaluation of the Impact of Guardians ad Litem in Child Abuse or Neglect Judicial Proceedings*, prepared by CSR, Inc. (Washington, D.C.: 1988). For a review of existing U.S. research on this topic, see D.N. Duquette, "Independent Representation of Children in Protection Proceedings," in J. Hudson and B. Galaway (eds), *The State as Parent* Dordrecht: The Netherlands Kluwer Academic Publishers, 1989).

26. HHS, *National Evaluation*.

3
Program Structure

A successful child advocacy program requires a sound organizational structure and a defined, clearly accepted place in the local community. By far the most common means of providing representation for children in abuse and neglect cases is through private attorneys appointed by the juvenile court judge.[1] Existing statutes and court rules, tradition, and the authority of the court provide the sort of clear legitimacy for which lay child advocate programs should strive. Unfortunately the research indicates that appointment of private lawyers who receive no special training is the least satisfactory way to provide representation for children.[2]

A few communities support an office in which specialized staff attorneys represent children in protection cases and, often, youth accused of delinquency offenses. The effectiveness of such programs varies considerably, however, and formal training and standardized approaches to cases are unusual.[3] Nonetheless, increasing the number of lawyers specializing in child advocacy is a promising avenue for improving child representation in protection cases throughout the nation.

Programs that rely exclusively on lawyers to provide representation for children face the same issues of role ambiguity, barriers to advocacy, and the need for training, interdisciplinary consultation, and independence that confront a lay advocacy (CASA) program.

CASA Models

Dissatisfaction with existing forms of representation for children in child abuse and neglect cases has led to a search for alternative methods. CASA programs provide one set of alternatives. They used trained volunteers to perform various duties, including investigating cases, reporting observations to the court, and

---

Martha W. Steketee is the primary author of this chapter.

providing casework services in conjunction with court staff. Several national organizations have funded, supported, and encouraged the development of these programs over the past decade.[4] The National Court Appointed Special Advocate Association (NCASAA) was formed in 1982 to provide training, conferences, and other support to the burgeoning number of CASA programs nationwide. As of 1988, there were 271 CASA programs in forty-five U.S. states.[5]

The structures of the lay advocacy programs vary considerably. Court systems in different areas have different needs, judges differ in their perceptions of the value of volunteer advocates, and communities vary in the kinds of potential volunteers who are available. No consensus has yet emerged in favor of a particular form of a child advocacy office, although we propose a model which is outlined in appendix A.

The NCASAA describes four model program structures: CASA–Guardian ad litem, CASA and attorney team, friend of the court, and monitor. The advocate's duties in these models range from review of case paperwork, to advocacy in consultation with an attorney, to independent fact finding and advocacy. All of the models provide a different blend of advocate authority, responsibility, and teamwork, yet all provide the court with additional information to use in making decisions about services, placement, and other issues related to the child's interests. One major distinction among the models concerns the legal status of the volunteer as party or nonparty to the case. The CASA with official party status, conferred by statute or court rule, is entitled to full and independent participation in the legal proceedings. He or she can file motions, call witnesses, and take appeals. A nonparty role, on the other hand, is more limited and may depend on the discretion of the individual judge.

A 1986 NCASAA managment study revealed that over 50 percent of CASA programs functioning at that time had selected the guardian ad litem–party model; 30 percent were using the friend of the court model; 10 percent used the CASA and attorney team model; and less than 5 percent used the monitor model.[6]

CASA–Guardian Ad Litem

The CASA–guardian ad litem (GAL) model substitutues trained court-appointed volunteers for attorney GALs in child abuse and neglect proceedings.[7] Such programs usually are initiated by an interested judge, and the court generally assumes responsibility for program funding and administration under this model, although it may be run by a private nonprofit agency. Official court sanction confers the program with important status and support from court administration, community social service agencies, and attorneys.

In this model, the volunteer is a party to the case, entitled to examine witnesses, submit evidence, receive copies of all relevant materials from the court, and present independent petitions on behalf of the child represented. This model confers the most authority and responsibility on the advocate. In addition to the GAL, an attorney may be appointed to represent the child during certain court proceedings—for example, if a case goes to trial. The CASA-GAL acts as investigator, advocate, facilitator, and monitor of the proceedings relevant to the child's case.

CASA—Attorney Team

The CASA-attorney team model of volunteer advocacy programs calls for teamwork at each stage of the court proceedings. Under this model, the court appoints an attorney and a volunteer to represent the child together. The attorney provides consultation and legal direction to the volunteer, prepares all legal documents, and presents the case to the court based upon information and facts the volunteer has obtained. The volunteer investigates and evaluates the child's circumstances, identifies and advocates the child's interests, mediates among competing or conflicting points of view, and monitors and facilitates service delivery. This model most closely approximates the approach taken in this book and codified in appendix A.

Friend of the Court

Under the friend of the court program model, trained volunteers are appointed for individual cases at varying points in the case process, according to court discretion. The courts themselves may or may not provide funding for this program; frequently private sources, such as the National Council of Jewish Women or the Junior League, have provided initial funding and training resources to operate the program. This form of volunteer participation is more frequent in courts that appoint an attorney in addition to the volunteer for each case.

The volunteer friend of the court serves as a witness or impartial observer to case activities and is not regarded as a legal party to the case. This model allows the volunteer to act as information gatherer as well as monitor, free to conduct interviews of the parents and child, investigate case activity, and submit written reports.

Monitor

The monitor model gives the advocate the least legal standing as party to the case, but it is also the model with the most flexibility. Such programs serve at the pleasure of the court, usually in addition to a court-appointed attorney representing each child. The volunteer under this model serves as the eyes and ears of the court and acts a a case aide in reviewing case materials. The volunteer may take on many tasks within the court itself to help expedite cases (for example, monitoring legal files maintained on each child and drafting court orders). Such volunteers do not advocate in the courtroom but rather aid in the smooth flow of cases through the court process.

Community Issues in Program Development

Purposes

The purpose of volunteer child advocate programs is to serve the best interests of the child. Although this is a rather nebulous purpose statement, a number of concrete goals may be served by such programs.

Improved Representation. Research indicates that programs utilizing trained volunteers can provide better representation for children than systems relying exclusively on lawyers with no special training in this area.[8] Organizers should investigate the existing child protection system in their area to determine how volunteers can most usefully enter the local court process for protecting children. What kinds of volunteers are available? What duties for them will the court support? Careful training and supervision of the volunteers is key to their success in improving representation.

Improved Decision-Making. The volunteer advocate should be trained to question others involved in the child protection process, including parents, social workers, and attorneys. If there is no independent advocate for the child, the interests of the state or those of the parents can overwhelm case decision making. Since the independent advocate's only job is to ensure that the child's interests are considered and that all appropriate information about the case is put before the court, his or her representation can strongly affect the quality of the decisions the court is called upon to make.

Reduced Costs. A lay advocate who works cooperatively with an attorney may provide better representation for the child at the same or less cost than using attorneys alone. Because lawyers representing children are compensated out of state or local tax dollars at a rate below their fees for other services, they generally devote less time and effort to these cases, with predictable effects on the quality of the representation.[9] A CASA program with a small staff that supports and trains volunteer advocates may be able to stretch existing funds between specially trained lawyers and CASAs to improve child representation with no additional cost.

Increased Community Involvement and Awareness. A program utilizing community volunteers in the local juvenile or family court provides the added benefit of educating those adult citizens about the needs and interests of abused and neglected children. Community involvement in the juvenile court system provides an additional political base for the needs of children and youth, as well as an informed check on judges and other community leaders who may not be properly discharging their responsibility to children. Volunteer programs provide access to and involvement with the court and social system, and training for case advocacy may lead to other forms of advocacy for children.

Inside or Outside? Independence from the Courts and Agencies

Volunteer programs devoted to representing the interests of children in the courts have emerged because many think that children have not been given the care and attention they deserve by overburdened, understaffed, and underfunded juvenile and family court and child welfare systems. Should an advocate program be run as part of the court, where it could enjoy the support of a large and influential organization? Or should it be administratively independent of both the court and the social agencies so as to keep its advocacy free of control by others?

Some programs have originated as a project of an outside group and then become part of the court institution itself, with offices within the court building and run through county or city funding.[10] Other programs have originated in the court through the leadership of an innovative and powerful judge. The organizational and political support of the court is certainly an advantage to any program. Program planners and local officials, however, should discuss the short- and long-range structures of the programs on a continuous basis. If these volunteer advocacy programs are intended to provide an ongoing independent advocacy service as a means of improving services to children and their families, then the programs should be organized independently of both courts and social services agencies. The support of the judges and other community leaders is essential, however, as is their participation. The political support and expertise of judges, social service directors, and other community leaders can be obtained through their participation on boards of directors of an organization administratively independent of the court and other agencies.

Resistance by Local Agencies and Courts

Some in local agencies and courts may criticize an advocacy service as merely adding one more critical voice in the process without adding any meaningful services. The advocate's voice states another version of the best interests of the child, the criticism goes, but does not actually add services the child needs. Perhaps, it is argued, the funds used for advocacy could be better spent for additional social services, such as housing, jobss, medical care or casework staff. Given the unmet needs in a particular community, is an advocacy program the highest priority for receiving additional funds? Another criticism is that these well-meaning advocates do little but make work more difficult for the caseworkers. They ask for information, keep them on the telephone in conversation, and otherwise tax their ability to meet the needs of their caseload. Given these costs of vigorous advocacy, are there benefits to the community?

Clearly the answer is "yes." The voice of the child serves an important function in keeping the needs of the youngster prominently before busy professionals with many competing demands. A lay advocate with only a few cases can see to it that the child gets more individual attention than she might otherwise. Our social service system is extremely complex, with many different offices and professionals each providing only a portion of the necessary help to a family. With so many ingredients to a successful recipe for help, it is easy for a critical ingredient to be left out or provided late. The system may not follow through.

The advocate is at his or her best in nudging and cajoling the complex array of social services to come together in the right amounts and at the right time to assist the child and family. The advocate provides an additional check and balance to the system and increases the likelihood that it will work properly for a particular child.[11]

Advocacy Tone

The various program models offer different specific roles for the child advocate to perform. The friend of the court, GAL, and CASA-attorney models provide opportunities for the advocate to conduct independent assessments of particular cases. It should be remembered, however, that in each of the models, the volunteer advocate is but one of many voices attempting to articulate a child's best interests. Given that all the actors share this broad goal, a cooperative, problem-solving strategy generally provides the best results.

Many of the child advocacy models provide a range of opportunities for independent and team decision making by the court actors. Many times the advocate is tempted to become another adversarial party in the proceedings, but this stance or strategy toward voicing a particular conception of a child's interests encourages antagonism among the parties. The child advocate should advance the child's interest in protection proceedings in a cooperative, facilitative manner to the greatest extent possible.

Child advocates typically prefer a nonadversarial approach to these cases, and as long as all sides share a similar view of the problem and desired outcome, such as family reunification, a conciliation approach is likely to be successful. When, however, the parents, the child protection agency, and the child's advocate do not see the problem in the same terms or differ markedly on what the state intervention ought to be on behalf of the child, some means of resolving those conflicts must be used, and here the traditional due process procedures are appropriate for resolving the conflict. It is hoped that mediation and conciliation will be successful more often than not and that the proportion of cases in which the traditional adversarial approach is relied upon can be reduced to a small minority.

Lay Volunteers as Child Advocates

Given the responsibilities advocates are asked to shoulder, it is clear that some specialized training is needed to prepare those recruited to be child advocates. Assuming that an adequate training program is available, who should be trained to be a child advocate? What characteristics, skills, knowledge, and experience should an advocate have? Are professionals in law or mental health more capable than lay volunteers in performing the role of a child advocate?

Since child advocacy programs have only recently been introduced into juvenile and family courts, there is no single standard that determines who is qualified to be a child advocate. Attorneys are generally identified as the most legitimate group to serve as legal representatives for children in child protection proceedings by virtue of their knowledge of the law and their professional training in legal doctrine and procedures. The expense of hiring attorneys to represent children thoroughly in all child protection proceedings would be substantial, however. Consequently courts are increasingly permitting trained lay volunteers to function as the child's legal advocate.

We believe that the most efficient and effective mode of providing child advocacy services is to have attorneys specializing in child welfare law train and supervise lay volunteers, with consultation available as needed from other disciplines and from an organizational structure. Support for this model comes from several recent studies. A study that compared the effectiveness of three groups—attorneys, law students, and lay (nonlawyer) volunteers—in representing children in child protection cases found that trained lay volunteers were as effective as trained attorneys and law students and more effective than untrained attorneys.[12]

In June 1988 the U.S. Department of Health and Human Services released the most comprehensive evaluation to date on the performance of child representatives in child protection proceedings.[13] CSR, Incorporated, which conducted the evaluation, studied five types of representation models: a law student clinic model, a staff attorney model, a paid private attorney model, a lay volunteer–staff attorney model, and a lay volunteer model (with attorney and staff support). They looked at two examples of each model in nine counties in six different states. Data were gathered from three sources: interviews with judges, states attorneys, and caseworkers; records of the court and the child welfare agency; and two in-depth case studies from each site (called "network interviews"). The researchers concluded by not recommending the private attorney or the law student models. They recommended the staff attorney model but pointed out two disadvantages: little child contact and no postdispositional monitoring. They saved their highest recommendation for the two models employing lay advocates, which they found were characterized by thorough case investigation, highly involved advocates, frequent child contact, postdispositional monitoring, and obtaining appropriate services for the child. Although the CASA model had disadvantages—personal involvement of advocates possibly being too high, cases taking a longer time in the initial dispositional phase, and careful training being needed—the researchers highly recommended these models.

Recruitment

Many existing child advocacy programs began as volunteer community service projects, sponsored by community organizations such as the National Council of Jewish Women or professional organizations such as the National Council of Juvenile and Family Court Judges. We suggest that there is a definite advantage in recruiting lay volunteers from community-based groups. We propose that the membership of community-based organizations (such as church groups, organizations represented in community centers, and neighborhood groups) will most likely reflect the values and culture of the families appearing in court proceedings.

Students from neighboring universities and colleges also can be a valuable resource pool for recruiting child advocates. College students, particularly graduate students, generally are eager to learn and have the maturity and capacity to develop the skills necessary to be effective child advocates. In addition, they generally have more time than working adults do to offer volunteer services.

Mental health professionals provide another rich recruitment pool for child advocate programs. Mental health professionals (such as social workers, counselors, psychologists, psychiatrists, and clergy), have specialized knowledge in child development and/or experience in working with families, which can contribute greatly to the role of child advocate. Members of this group can also serve as support staff or consultants to lay volunteers, significantly strengthening the quality of child advocacy services provided to children.

Length and Intensity of Service

Programs must determine the length and intensity of service required of their child advocates. Traditional legal representation often is provided on a hearing-by-hearing basis, without assurance that a representative will continue with a case to its termination in the court process. Many volunteer programs, however, require at least a one-year commitment from their advocates and assign advocates to stay with a case throughout the court process. This ideal provides the continuity necessary for adequate monitoring of the case, as well as consistency for the child.

Conclusion

Volunteer performance should be evaluated within the context of the representation that the court would otherwise provide. In most cases, this option is private attorney representation. The potential child advocacy program should consider the benefits and costs of a volunteer program in its jurisdiction. Empirical research and impressionistic data show that properly trained and supervised volunteers can do at least as well as trained attorneys, and better than untrained attorneys, in representing children in protection proceedings.[14]

Notes

1. U.S. Health and Human Services (HHS), *National Evaluation of the Impact of Guardians ad Litem in Child Abuse or Neglect Judicial Proceedings*, prepared by CSR, Inc. (Washington, D.C.: Administration on Children, Youth and Families, 1988).

2. Ibid.

3. Ibid.

4. Some primary sponsors are the National Council of Juvenile and Family Court Judges, the National Council of Jewish Women, and the Office of Juvenile Justice and Delinquency Prevention.

5. *National Court Appointed Special Advocate Association, 1987–88 Annual Report*, (Seattle: National CASA Association, 1989).

6. Benjamin, *CASA: A Guide to Program Development*, revised and ed. Miriam Pace Longino (Seattle: NCASAA, 1988). The following discussion is based on NCASAA materials and other published sources. Additional program materials are available directly from the National Court Appointed Special Advocate Association, 2722 Eastlake Ave. E., Suite 220, Seattle, Washington 98102; (206-328-8588). Many states have their own associations of CASA programs for information and referral, for example, Michigan Association of Court Appointed Special Advocates, 115 West Allegan, Suite 500, Lansing, Michigan 48933; (517)482-7533. The NCASAA publishes a directory of CASA programs.

7. *Guardian ad litem* is a broad legal term referring to an individual officially appointed by a court to provide a range of types of representation in court proceedings. The term can apply to those appointed to represent the interests of individuals who are in some way incapacitated (for example, by old age, mental condition, or youth). In this book, GAL is used to indicate someone appointed to represent the interests of children in abuse and neglect proceedings.

8. HHS, *National Evaluation*; D.N. Duquette and S.H. Ramsey, "Representation of Children in Child Abuse and Neglect Cases: An Empirical Look at What Constitutes Effective Representation," *University of Michigan Journal of Law Reform* (1987) 20: 341–408; D.N. Duquette and S.H. Ramsey, "Using Lay Volunteers to Represent Children in Child Protection Court Proceedings," *Child Abuse and Neglect: The International Journal* 10:2 (1986): 293–308.

9. Note, "The Non-Attorney Guardian Ad Litem in Child Abuse and Neglect Proceedings: The King County, Washington Experience," *Washington Law Review* 58' (1983): 853–870.

10. One example of this transformation from outside to inside the system is the CASA program (friend of the court model) in St. Louis County, Missouri. This program began as a project funded solely by the National Council of Jewish Women and developed into one funded in part by the county.

11. We have little empirical support, however, for the proposition that effective

advocacy improves service delivery to a specific child or his or her family. More research needs to be done on this and other questions regarding child advocacy.

12. Duquette and Ramsey, "Representation of Children."

13. HHS, *National Evaluation*.

14. D.N. Duquette and S.H. Ramsey, "Representation of Children" and "Using Lay Volunteers."

4

Identifying the Best Interests of the Child

The central concern of the child advocate—as, presumably, of all those involved in a child protection proceeding—is with the child's "best interests." Yet few other concepts are so difficult to define and so imbued with subjective and fallible judgment as this one. Any decision about what is best for a particular child, or for children in general, must be based on two sets of factors that are fundamentally indeterminate: those having to do with predicting outcomes and those having to do with values.[1]

Anyone asked to make a decision regarding children is faced with having to predict both the short- and long-term consequences of any action, usually on the basis of limited information regarding both the child and the available alternatives. The information is not only limited but often changes in significant and unpredictable ways—for instance, when an imprisoned father is released and seeks custody of the child or when a previously supportive relative becomes unwilling or unable to continue that degree of support. Given the constantly shifting nature of these cases and the fact that even professionals who study child development do not agree on what actions lead reliably to particular outcomes, a degree of speculation must often substitute for knowledge.

The second problem is one of values: on what basis do we determine the child's best interests: material well-being? emotional security? educational opportunity? A little thought makes clear that such decisions come down to judgments, as one writer has put it, about the "purposes and values of life itself."[2] While there may be some cases in which the child's best interest is clear to all—for instance, temporary removal from a situation of immediate, indisputable harm—such cases are probably the exception, not the rule.

This chapter was written by David Murphey.

Historical and Cultural Perspectives

To forewarn further the prospective advocate of the elusiveness of any easy or absolute definition of what is best for the child, both cross-cultural evidence and the historical record of our own society underscore the relativity of such judgments. Attitudes toward children, expressed in how they are treated by their parents, as well as in how their best interests are conceived, have changed (and continue to change) to reflect the needs and values of the adult world.[3]

In Western culture, until the late sixteenth century, infants were considered to be little different from "noisy animals," to be socialized as expediently as possible and, if necessary (often inevitably), abandoned or even killed.[4] After the age of six or seven, they were assumed to be the equals of adults in terms of sharing in their activities (and adversities), though they were not accorded rights of their own since they remained essentially property of their parents.[5] The modern view of childhood as a relatively prolonged time of special vulnerability, requiring adult sensitivity and protection, was foreign to this earlier era.

There are, however, some important continuities from earlier times. Where the child's interests are concerned, there is a presumption, which in Western tradition dates back to antiquity, of parental rights.[6] By law as well as by social standard, parents are presumed both to desire and in fact to act on behalf of what is in their child's best interest. These presumptive parental rights include, broadly, the rights to care, custody, and control of their children. The burden is on the state to demonstrate, in a particular case, that such rights should be abridged. It is important to keep in mind, too, that historically when the state has intervened to limit parental rights, its concern has not been to protect children or their rights but to uphold the interests of society—for example, to protect it from the consequences of an idle, undisciplined work force or, in our own time, to compel adherence to minimally acceptable community standards of care. Children's rights have typically been defined negatively, in relation to parent behavior that falls below the acceptable minimum standard (the right not to be gravely neglected or abused, for example) rather than in absolute terms (the right to adequate care, appropriate education, and so forth).[7]

A cross-cultural perspective forces the view that there is no universal standard for the child's best interests, for what constitutes "good" or "bad" treatment.[8] Ethnographic study has made clear not only the variety of parenting practices and societal attitudes toward children but also the importance of judging any behavior within a holistic cultural context. For instance, in many subsistence agricultural societies, children at age seven or eight typically assume many adult roles, such as child care, housework, and field labor, often without direct adult supervision. Furthermore, in many preliterate or preindustrial societies, children undergo certain initiation rites that signify their entry into adult life, and such practices commonly include ritual scarification or mutilation. Other cultures would regard such treatment as brutal abuse, but within the culture where it is customary and expected, parents' failure to perform such practices would be seen as serious neglect. Nor are we in Western industrialized countries immune from unfavorable judgment by outsiders. For example, while most of us believe it is important for children to sleep apart from their parents, such a practice seems not only strange but harmful in the eyes of traditional Hawaiians; they believe such isolation of children is both developmentally unwise and potentially dangerous, and children sleep together with parents—if not in the same bed, then at least in the same room.[9]

Appreciation of the cultural context in understanding what is best for children is important not only in the abstract but also for how we respond to ethnic diversity within our own communities. The child advocate needs to make an effort to identify the local community standards for the upbringing of its children. If the advocate is not a member of the community to which the child belongs, he or she should ascertain such standards by talking with those who are, such as protective services workers, other social workers, judges assigned to child protection cases, as well as neighbors or family members. These informants can help put into perspective the facts of a case by distinguishing what is considered aberrant or normal in that community.

To be aware of the relativism of judgments of the child's best interests is not, however, to accept any treatment of children that can be placed in a context of community practice. Any practices that result in objective harm, either physical or psychological, must be judged by a single non-ethnocentric standard. Virtually all cultures share a conviction that children may not be harmed, and it is that standard that the advocate can most usefully uphold rather than focusing on practices that themselves are so culturally diverse and so entrenched.[10] It may also be useful to point out that some practices (scarification rites, for example) that may carry a positive meaning in one culture may have to be adapted or even dropped once they are transplanted, if they are likely to be judged unsympathetically by the laws of the dominant society.

Family Autonomy versus State Intervention

Once a child has gained the recognition of the legal system, as in a protection hearing, he or she is at risk from two different directions: overintervention and underintervention. If a court fails to recognize a home situation that seriously endangers the child and underintervenes by returning him or her to the home without taking adequate protective action, the child may be harmed, or even killed, by the parents' abuse or neglect. On the other hand, if the court overintervenes by unnecessarily assuming jurisdiction or removing the child, the child (and the rest of the family) may suffer a serious disruption of family life, and the child may be subject to a new kind of neglect or abuse within the system.

A number of larger issues are foreshadowed here. What are the rights of families to privacy and autonomy versus the right of the state to intervene on behalf of a child? Should families be preserved at all costs? Should the state intervene at the slightest risk to a child? These are questions not easily answered, if indeed they can be definitively answered at all. These questions are perhaps even more difficult in the United States, where the tension between individual autonomy and society's needs as a whole has been historically everpresent.

Here we simply want to raise such questions and offer a couple of perspectives. Recently it has been recognized that the tendency toward the modern therapeutic state carries with it a dangerous paradox: as the state increasingly seeks (presumably benevolently) to regulate individuals, its faith in the wisdoms of professional intervention tends to emphasize the needs rather than the rights of those it seeks to aid. Professionals intent on "doing good" can thus deny the possibility of conflict between themselves and their clients, and so justify nearly any intervention.[11]

That caution notwithstanding, a second view is to consider not only what is in the best interests of either the individual or the family but the interests of a whole functioning social system.[12] Perhaps the value we place on individual and family independence contributes to a high—and more potentially harmful— threshold for intervention. If we were to value interdependence and integration more, rather than isolation and privacy, then perhaps the alternatives would not be either family autonomy or state intervention but the provision of social supports designed to strengthen family and community life before abuse or neglect occurs.

Practical Issues in Intervention

1. In most cases children need to maintain the physical and psychological bonds with their families, even when those families have significant problems.

2. If a separation from the family is necessary, the child should be placed in most homelike alternative setting, and the aim should be early family reunification.

3. A child's experience of time is different from an adult's and demands that decisions affecting him or her be made promptly.

We treat these issues in greater detail in chapter 6, where specific roles and responsibilities of the advocate are discussed.

Notes

1. R. Mnookin, *In the Interest of Children: Advocacy Law Reform and Public Policy* (New York: W.H. Freeman and Company, 1985).

2. Ibid.

3. C.J. Ross, "The Lessons of the Past: Defining and Controlling Child Abuse in the United States," in Gerbner, Rother, and Zigler, eds., *Child Abuse: An Agenda for Action*

(New York: Oxford University Press, 1980); B.G. Fraser, "The Child and His Parents: A Delicate Balance of Rights, in Helfer and Kempe, eds., *Child Abuse and Neglect: The Family and the Community* (Cambridge, Mass.: Ballinger, 1976).

4. Ross, "Lessons of the Past." See also Philippe Ariés, *Centuries of Childhood: A Social History of Family Life*, trans. Robert Baldick (New York: Vintage Books, 1962).

5. Fraser, "Child and His Parents."

6. Ibid.

7. Ibid.; Ross, "Lessons of the Past."

8. J. Korbin, "Child Abuse and Neglect: The Cultural Context," in Helfer and Kempe, eds., *The Battered Child*, 4th ed. (Chicago: University of Chicago Press, 1987).

9. Ibid.

10. Ibid.

11. Ross, "Lessons of the Past."

12. J. Garbarino et al., "Who Owns the Children? An Ecological Perspective on Public Policy Affecting Children" in *Child and Youth Services* in *Legal Reforms Affecting Child and Youth Services*, G.B. Mellon, ed. (Haworth Press, 1982, 43–63).

5
The Child's Voice in Identifying the Advocate's Goals

What voice ought the child have in identifying his or her interests and the goals of the advocacy? Among the difficult issues facing a child advocate, few others are as troublesome as whether the advocate ought to pursue the child's interests as identified by the child or pursue the best interests of the child as defined by the advocate. Partly because of the child's immaturity and partly because the child is a unique and separate individual with personal wants and views, the child's opinion of what would be a good outcome is not always the same as what the advocate thinks would be a good outcome. Differences between advocate and client are quite common when an adult is the client, and in such cases the advocate nearly always defers to the goals set forth by the client. But because of the child's age and because adults often discount children's views, it is easy for the child's advocate to assume a paternalistic role and assert the advocate's own judgment over the child's expressed wishes.

When the child is very young (under seven for instance), it is easier to resolve any conflict between the advocate and the child client. Because the youngest children often cannot articulate even a preference in important questions such as temporary placement and ultimate custody, the advocate nearly always determines the interests of the child and the goals of the advocacy. Similarly, the conflict is easier to resolve when the youngster is older. We may not agree with a fifteen, sixteen, or seventeen year old, but most of us respect their right to an opinion and to have the court hear that opinion. The conflict is especially problematic, however, in the middle years, from seven to fourteen, for instance, when the child is of an age where he or she is articulate but may lack mature judgment. A hypothetical example illustrates the dilemma:

> Max is ten years old. The protective service worker alleges that his father has beaten him severely and has locked him in his room for long periods. Max's mother lives several states away and is unavailable to care for

David Murphey contributed substantially to this chapter.

him, but his father's brother lives nearby and has offered to allow Max to live with him. Protective services thinks the uncle would provide a safe and caring environment. Max, however, states that he prefers to stay with his father ("if he doesn't beat me so much, and he says he won't"). What should the child's representative recommend regarding placement?

The issue is complicated by the fact that there is more involved here than simply a child's immaturity. The advocate for the child must keep in mind that any wishes the child expresses in this situation may be colored, on the one hand, by guilt, loyalty conflicts, or fears of potential retribution, and, on the other, by anger at parents that may be unrelated to the specific alleged abuse—for instance, over a parental divorce or stemming from an adolescent's need to establish independence.

Despite a child's young age and relative immaturity, however, a number of considerations argue in favor of the advocate's representing the child's own expressed wishes rather than the advocate's conceptions of the child's best interests.[1] Primarily, taking such a position may provide a counterweight to those of the other actors in the proceedings, all of whom presume to act in the child's best interests but who often have strong interests of their own that may not be congruent with the child's. In addition, representing the child's own wishes may help to counteract the cultural and class biases prevalent in many protection proceedings. Finally, there is an ethical argument that the child deserves respect as an individual rather than paternalism (however well intentioned).

Judges may find it easier to make better decisions if the child's judgment is among the views strongly presented to the court. The court need not accept the position put forth by the advocate in each case, but at least the youngster's voice is presented and heard.

Consider, in the case of a middle-years child or older, that many persons in the child protection process are charged with pursuing the "best interests of the child." The child protection worker has initiated the action in the best interests of the child; the agency attorney or the prosecuting attorney presses the case in the best interests of the of the child; the parents and their attorney will often frame their defenses in terms of the best interests of the child; and, ultimately, the judge will make a legal determination in the best interests of the child. If the advocate does not speak up for the child and express and argue for the child's stated wishes, no one else is likely to do so.

Giving Voice to the Older Child's Wishes

The American Bar Association recommends that when the young person is "capable of considered judgment on his or her behalf," the advocate (lawyer) should defer to the youngster in determining the objectives of the proceedings.

That is, deciding the goals to be sought should remain the client's responsibility after full consultation with counsel.[2] The Model Rules of Professional Conduct for lawyers also seem to anticipate some of the subtle problems in representing children. They provide that a lawyer shall abide by a client's decisions concerning the objectives of the representation.[3] Model Rule 1.14 provides:

> (a) When a client's ability to make adequately considered decisions in connection with the representation is impaired, whether because of *minority*, mental disability or for some other reason, the lawyer shall, as far as reasonably possible, maintain a normal client-lawyer relationship with the client.[4] (emphasis added)

The comment to this rule says, in part:

> Furthermore, to an increasing extent, the law recognizes intermediate degrees of competence. For example, children as young as five or six years of age, and certainly those of ten or twelve, are regarded as having opinions that are entitled to weight in legal proceedings regarding custody.[5]

Nevertheless, in many situations the advocate may reasonably be in doubt as to whether a child has the cognitive and/or emotional capability to express personal wishes based on a reasoned understanding of the situation. Attorneys' professional codes do not explicitly refer to age as a criterion that should influence their treatment of their clients but rather consider factors such as the client's capacity to understand the situation and to direct counsel. The pace of development and level of maturity vary from child to child; youngsters have sufficient ability at various ages. How, then, is a child's competence to be judged by the advocate?

One writer has proposed that the child's ability to make a thoughtful decision depends on his or her abilities to understand, to reason, and to communicate, together with having a set of values.[6] Assessing these abilities is bound to be somewhat subjective; however, a review of developmental research suggests that as early as the age of seven, children begin to show some decision-making ability that is consistent with these standards. For example, they can consider cause and effect, use information, reason about alternatives, and communicate the decision they have made. Children at this age, however, do lack many intellectual capacities, including abstract thinking and an adult sense of time. For the advocate, the practical implication of these findings is that the representative must assess the child's cognitive ability, emotional maturity, language development, and amount of information and experience with respect to the particular decision to be made. While the age seven guideline may be useful in making an initial presumption of a child's competence, individuals will vary greatly. There can be no substitute for the advocate's sensitive and informed assessment.

Proposal

In the proposal for legislation set forth in appendix A, we recommend that at age fourteen the child should be presumed capable of determining his or her own interests and that the advocate should be required to represent the child's wishes in those cases. (The choice of fourteen is somewhat arbitrary, much as drawing lines at sixteen for a driver's licenses and twenty-one for purchasing alcohol. It strikes a balance, however, between a child's right to self-determination and a child's need for guidance and protection.) A presumption of the child's capacity to determine his or her own interests means that unless the youngster is suffering from a serious deficiency because of very low intelligence or mental or emotional disability, the advocate listens to the child and, after a period of private counseling and discussion with him or her, vigorously pursues the child's point of view in the court and out of court with the other participants in the child protection process.

Younger children may be mature enough to direct the advocate's goals, and advocates should make a case-by-case determination in this matter. When a child possesses the proper maturity, the advocate should defer to the youngster in determining the goals of the advocacy. In every case and at every age, the child's point of view should be considered by the advocate, of course. Sometimes it is in the child's best interests, regardless of age and maturity, to have the point of view presented clearly and vigorously to the court.

To allay the anxiety that a child may feel at taking full responsibility for the decision, the advocate should help the child of any age understand that it is the judge, not the child, who will finally decide, though the child's own wishes may be made known and will be considered.

There is a risk, of course, that advocates will find they are obliged to pursue goals with which they do not personally agree. Lawyers have that difficult experience regularly. When the child is granted some rights of self-determination, the advocate is required to sublimate personal views in favor of the older child's wishes.

Since lay volunteers do not share the tradition of sublimating personal views in favor of the client's wishes, they may give less weight to the child's point of view than lawyers would. If a program adopts a policy that youngsters at some age deserve to have their wishes pursued by the advocate, careful training and supervision is essential. Persons unwilling or unable to take an advocacy position unless they personally agree with it should be transferred to another case when disagreements between advocate and child client arise.

Conclusion

Disagreements between the advocate and the child regarding the goals of the advocacy do not occur frequently. They do arise, however, and the advocate needs to be prepared for this difficult choice. We recommend that the advocate respond differently to three separate ages: the very young child, the older child, and the middle years child from seven to fourteen. The weight given to the child's wishes will vary with the youngster's age and maturity. The advocate will always consider the stated wishes of the child in formulating goals and will presume, after proper discussion and counseling, that the wishes of a child will be determinative at age fourteen.

Notes

1. S.H. Ramsey, "Representation of the Child in Protection Proceedings: The Determination of Decision-Making Capacity," *Family Law Quarterly* 17 (1983): 287.

2. American Bar Association, Institute of Judicial Administration, Juvenile Justice Standards, *Standards Relating to Counsel for Private Parties* (Cambridge, Mass.: Ballinger Publishing Company, 1980): §3.1(b)(ii).

3. *Model Rules of Professional Conduct*, 1.2(a).

4. Rule 1.14(a).

5. Ibid.

6. Ramsey, "Representation of the Child."

6
Dimensions of Child Advocacy

*C*hild advocacy describes a system or program activity that seeks to ensure the provision of services for children. The word *advocacy,* from the Latin, means to speak on behalf of someone or something. Child advocacy encompasses the idea of children's rights and is based on the concept that every child is entitled to the care and services needed for optimum growth and development. In our society, not all parents or caretakers have the means or abilities to provide adequately for their children, and some parents mistreat their children through direct action or inaction. In this context, child advocacy can be performed by an agency, person, or institution that seeks to promote children's interests and to protect their rights in many different settings, including the home, courts, schools, and social agencies. In case advocacy, the individual advocate works to ensure needed services to specific families and children. In class advocacy, the individual advocate focuses on changing procedures, personnel, or laws as they may affect categories or groups of families and children.

Roles and Responsibilities of the Child Advocate

The major roles the child advocate performs reflect the advocate's unique position as an independent representative of the child's best interests (figure 6–1):

1. Fact finder–investigator.
2. Legal representative.
3. Case monitor.
4. Mediator–conciliator.
5. Information and resource broker (that is, a critical consumer of information).

Karin Elliott contributed substantially to this chapter, and a portion was written by Martha W. Steketee.

As fact finder, the child advocate employs investigative skills to obtain from all parties involved in the case information and opinions regarding the child's well-being and the family's functioning. As legal representative, the child advocate provides counsel to child clients regarding the legal process, advises clients of recommendations for court action, and provides child clients with legal representation before the court. As case monitor, the child advocate takes active steps to ensure that the case is moving swiftly through the court process while properly serving the best interests of the child. As mediator-conciliator, the child advocate facilitates a collaborative working relationship among all parties so that problems can be resolved and a generally acceptable agreement can be presented to the court. Finally, as information and resource broker the child advocate identifies resource people and support services available in the community to assist the child and family in assessing problems, resolving conflicts, and strengthening family relationships.

In performing these roles, the child advocate must accomplish several tasks that often arise at each stage of the court process. The following section provides a conceptual framework that organizes tasks into process dimensions reflecting each role performed by the child advocate. We are presenting an ideal model that we feel can be adapted to meet the specific needs of particular court systems.

Process Dimensions of Child Advocacy: A Framework for Defining Tasks

The multiple dimensions to child advocacy unfold as the advocate steers a child protection case through the court process. The following process dimensions capture the essence of the child advocate's role:

1. Investigation.
2. Consultation.
3. Assessment.
4. Identifying the child's interests.
5. Permanency planning.
6. Client counseling.
7. Decision making.
8. Problem solving and mediation.
9. Identifying action steps.
10. Following up on action steps.

These tasks, which characterize the child advocacy process, can be categorized under the five roles performed by the child advocate (figure 6–1). The tasks can also be thought of as dimensions of child advocacy that are implemented in

Figure 6-1. Roles and Tasks of the Child Advocate

Fact Finder	Legal Representative	Case Monitor

investigation   identification of interests   permanency planning
consultation   client counseling   identification of action steps
assessment   decision making   follow-up
    consultation
    identification of action steps
    follow-up

Mediator	Information-Resource Broker

mediation   investigation
consultation   consultation
identification of action steps   identification of interests
decision making   mediation

Figure 6-2. Dimensions of Child Advocacy in the Child Protection Legal Process

Preliminary Hearing	Pretrial Conference	Trial	Dispositional Hearing	Review Hearings	Permanency Planning Hearing

DIMENSIONS

Investigation
Consultation
Assessment
Identifying the child's interests
Permanency planning
Client counseling
Decision making
Problem solving
Identifying action steps
Follow-up

varying ways during each stage of the legal process—typically, preliminary hearing, pretrial conference, trial, dispositional hearing, and review hearings (figure 6–2).

Part II of this book provides a step-by-step guide through the court process using these ten dimensions of child advocacy as a conceptual framework to assist child advocates in organizing their activities at each stage. A case example will be presented to illustrate the multiple roles child advocates perform throughout the court process. Through this case example, it will become clear that although each dimension is present at each stage, the dimensions of child advocacy vary in importance and prominence at various points of the legal process.

The advocate should appreciate the importance of suspending judgment until the facts are gathered and the case is assessed (dimensions one through six). A course of action should be tentatively identified before taking specific action steps (dimension seven-decision-making). Tentative positions will be raised and discussed (dimension eight-problem solving and mediating) before action is necessary (dimension nine-identifying action steps). In practice, these steps may be taken quite rapidly. The ten-step process described here may take an hour or more to read and discuss, but it may occur in minutes on some cases. Thinking about this as a linear, step-by-step approach may help organize the advocate's tasks, however.

The conversations in which the roles and dimensions are fulfilled occur in quite ordinary and commonplace physical settings. Much of the work will be done in brief exchanges in the hallways and waiting rooms of the court or in a conference room or office of the court or social service agency. The advocate will make personal visits to the foster home and, with permission from their lawyer, the home of the parents. Much can be accomplished in the later stages of the legal process by telephone. Although several hours of study and discussion are needed to acquire the habits of mind reflected in the dimensions, once they are mastered, the advocate may be able to implement the process in a relatively short time in many cases.

Investigation

What are the facts? What did someone see, hear, smell, taste, and feel to make him or her think that a particular child is abused or neglected? Who saw what, when and where?

Fact finding is one of the most important tasks during the initial stages of a child abuse or neglect case, particularly in the preliminary hearing and pretrial phases. During the preliminary hearing phase, the child advocate must obtain enough information to form a good understanding of the family's circumstances, so that a fair assessment can be made regarding the validity of the charges in the petition. Gathering information, however, is an ongoing processs that should continue as long as the child remains under court jurisdiction. Family circumstances may change, or new information may be disclosed at any time that may affect the well-being of the child and the status of the case.

Child advocates can employ several strategies to obtain information about suspected abuse or neglect. First, the court documents themselves should be reviewed. The initial piece of information available to advocates is the court petition, the legal document that briefly describes the alleged abuse or neglect under state statutes. The child advocate must make a conscious and careful effort to understand the nature of the allegations and to assess their accuracy and validity. Decisions arrived at regarding the acceptance of allegations made in the petition and the initial placement of the child clearly set a precedent for future decisions regarding child placement and family intervention. Therefore, the petition should be clearly understood and considered by child advocates during preliminary investigations and assessments concerning the child's well-being and family's functioning.

Second, direct interviewing of the parties allows advocates to make an independent assessment of the family situation. When the child advocate is acting as part of a CASA-attorney team, legal ethics require that the advocate get permission of the parents' attorney before speaking directly with the parents.

Third, since several other investigators gather information about the alleged abuse or neglect (among them protective service workers, Department of Social Service attorneys, court-appointed investigators, and attorneys for the parent[s]), child advocates can obtain additional information and clarify inconsistencies or gaps in information by comparing notes with these sources. Fourth, advocates can request that court-ordered professional assessments be completed if it is determined that additional information is necessary or could provide significant insight regarding the child's well-being. Since child advocates do not have the task of making a case for or against the abuse or neglect petition, they are in a unique position that allows them to investigate objectively the family situation and how it affects the child.

Questions of fact arise at every stage of the court process (that is, what happened, by whom, when?). To analyze the case, the advocate must begin with an accurate understanding of the facts. Fist, the advocate gets the information, then analyzes it, and then acts upon it.

Consultation

The advocate must also gather views and perspectives of others as to what should happen to the child and family under the circumstances. In consultation, the advocate seeks out the opinions and attitudes of the other major participants in the process. Talking with social workers, police officers, parents, children, individuals offering temporary foster care for the children, and other parties can provide advocates with a wealth of knowledge, information, and insight. The exchange of information, views, and perspectives can help the advocate to identify the presenting problems, clarify inconsistencies in information shared, and seek suggestions for solutions.

The advocate may have access to consulting professionals as part of a child advocate office or team. He or she may seek consultation and direction from his or her own laywer, social worker, psychologist, or psychiatrist who are not otherwise involved in the particular case except through the child advocate.

Consultation can take many forms. The advocate may make good use of the telephone and converse with the relevant persons on a regular basis. Advocates can organize case conferences to facilitate the exchange of information and perspectives, to identify points of agreement and disagreement, and to generate alternative courses of action. Other methods of consultation include client home visits, contact with resource people from agencies involved in the case, and written correspondence (for example, sharing written reports and assessments). Consultation keeps important lines of communication open and facilitates progress on the case between court appearances.

Assessment

Next, the child advocate needs to determine whether an informed understanding of the family and its problems exists among those who influence the court intervention process—attorneys, court-assigned worker, referee, or judge. Before a problem situation can be remedied, it must be identified accurately. If an assessment by a physician, psychologist, or other professional could add to the understanding of the problem, the advocate should suggest it—to the other parties and eventually to the court.

In addition to gathering and critically reviewing case assessments made by all parties, the child advocate should encourage parties to exchange and discuss their assessments and insights of the family situation. Except in emergency situations, the social worker should be able to provide a thorough assessment of the case and a reasonable plan for intervention. At each stage of the legal process the advocate must ask: What are the remaining questions? Is other information or expert evaluation required? On what evidence are current positions and recommendations based? Is the child at risk of physical or emotional harm? What is the degree of risk?

The child advocate continually is called upon to evaluate others' assessments and to make independent assessments regarding the family's situation and the child's well-being. Critical areas requiring thorough assessment are the strengths the weaknesses of the family, the social and psychological needs of the child, and whether the child is receiving at least minimally adequate food, clothing, shelter, guidance, and supervision.

Identifying the Child's Interests

Some common situations or circumstances clearly represent the best interests of most children in child protection cases most of the time:

1. Protection from physical and emotional harm.

2. Assurance of minimally adequate food, clothing, shelter, guidance, and supervision.

3. Provision of the least disruption to the youngster's normal living arrangements.

4. Placement in the most familiar, predictable, and consistent surroundings (for example, residing with relatives) when remaining in the home is not possible.

5. Consideration of a child's sense of time in the advocate's pursuit of prompt and efficient handling of each case.

6. Provision of reasonable and timely efforts for reunification of the family in the event that the child has been removed.

Some interests of the child may be overlooked by all but the child's advocate. Protection from physical and emotional harm and provision of minimally adequate food, clothing, shelter, guidance, and supervision are certainly in the child's best interests. The social worker and the court generally address these obvious deficiencies in the child's care even without vigorous advocacy by an independent child advocate. Other interests are more subtle, however, and may be overlooked by all but the child's representative.

The state intervention itself presents risks to the child. A child ordinarily has an interest in continuing to live with his or her parent(s), if at all possible, consistent with well-being and safety. An advocate can ensure that all reasonable efforts are taken to protect the child in the home rather than placing him or her out of familiar surroundings. The concept of a child's sense of time should be uppermost in the advocate's mind. Prompt and efficient handling of the case ordinarily benefits the child. If the child is to be removed from the family, the removal should be for the shortest time possible as long as the long-range plan remains reunification of the family.

Placement should generally be one that is the most familiar to the child (the least restrictive, most family-like setting). Contact with the family should ordinarily be maintained through regular visits. If services to the child and family are necessary before reunification (as long as reunification remains the goal), they should be identified accurately and provided promptly.

The interests of an individual child are not always consistent with the interests of the state agency. The state and county agencies must spread limited resources over many cases. For instance, when a child advocate urges that an eighteen-month-old client in foster case have visits with her mother every day, the social worker may respond, "We do not have the resources to arrange daily visits for all the children in foster care." The case advocate for the individual child can respond, "I appreciate how busy you are. I am not asking you to arrange daily visits for all children in foster care. But my client really needs it. I am asking you to do it just for her."

Because of high caseloads, agencies may be unwilling or unable to meet each child's individual needs (for example, for frequent visitation or for prompt psychological exams). An overburdened caseworker may not be as sensitive, as careful, or as skilled in judgment as she or he would be under less taxing circumstances. Consequently the child runs the risk of being inappropriately separated from familiar surroundings or of having an inadequate assessment of the home situation, so that remedies prescribed may be inappropriate, inadequate, or too late. A child removed from home runs the risk of being placed in multiple foster homes, of being abused in foster care, of being placed in inappropriate institutions, and of not having visits with parents and other family often enough.

Reasonable case plans may be developed by social agencies but not implemented properly or quickly, thus adding to the length of time the child is out of the home and lessening the child's chances of ever returning there.

Thus, though the best interests of any particular child are subjective and not precisely determinable, those we have identified are common to the vast majority of children and may be overlooked without an active child advocate.

Permanency Planning

The ultimate permanency planning goal is to provide children with a stable and secure home environment as soon as possible. Perhaps the most critical decision in the child protection process is whether to place the child outside the home at all. Even at the preliminary hearing, advocates should keep their eye on the long-term consequences to the child of any placement decision. The advocate should determine where the child's home is and whether that home is safe. What reasonable efforts can be made to prevent or eliminate the need for placing the child outside the home? If a child needs to be removed from his or her home, the advocate should ensure that the court try to identify a placement that is least disruptive to the child's normal living arrangement. Can the child be placed in a relative's or a friend's home? Can the child remain in the same neighborhood and/or in the same school? What is the quality of alternative placements?

If placement is necessary, it is imperative that the advocate get some estimate as to how long such a placement is likely to continue. Throughout the child's court involvement, it is essential to keep in mind the child's sense of time and the advantage, in most cases, of keeping placement outside the home as short as possible. When the children cannot be returned to their homes in a reasonable period of time, immediate steps should be taken to arrange alternative permanent homes for these children—perhaps through termination of parental rights and adoption.

Client Counseling

The primary purpose of the advocate's provision of client counseling is to ascertain and clarify the wishes of the child, provide legal advice, and be a consistent source of support to the child client throughout the process. Although the wishes of the child at any age are considered and given greater weight as the child gains in maturity, experience, and judgment, we assume that the best interests of the child are generally served when the advocate allows the youngster of fourteen to identify his or her own interests in the proceedings, thus setting the child advocate's goals.

Children brought into the court process are often confused, uncertain, and fearful. They usually do not understand what is happening to them and their families. They do not know whom they should trust with their feelings and with whom they can share their needs. For example, children may have preferences about where they want to live, but they are often unsure about the power they have to influence this decision. Advocates should let their child clients know that the advocate's role is to voice the child's needs and to represent his or her interests before the court; however, it should be made clear to the child that the judge or referee makes the final decisions about placement and the need for court intervention. Clarifying the respective roles and responsibilities of the child advocate and the judge, as well as explaining the degree to which a child can influence the court's decision, will help children deal with loyalty conflicts, guilt feelings, or fears about potential punishment for exposing family secrets.

Client counseling can be successful only when advocates develop enough of a relationship with their young clients so that they can adequately explain to the child what to expect of the court process, assess the child's understanding of the court involvement, and clarify the child's expressed wishes regarding the outcome of the case. The counseling process often is complex. While child advocates can do some explaining and try to clarify the child's wishes and preferences, they should be careful to avoid serious psychological counseling. If counseling is needed, the advocate's responsibility is to recommend to the court that psychological services be made available. The primary purpose of the advocate's provision of client counseling is to ascertain the wishes of the child, to provide legal advice, and to be a consistent source of support and information to the child client while proceeding through the legal system.

Decision Making

After gathering information and consulting with the child, the social worker, parents, and others who may have knowledge of or an interest in the child's welfare, the advocate should make some decisions, which may be tentative or preliminary. The advocate will be called upon to make recommendations to the court on behalf of the child. What position is the advocate going to take on behalf of the child? What are the goals for this procedural stage? What long-term goals can be identified given the information available thus far? Should previous decisions or positions be reevaluated or changed based on new information? The advocate should be as specific as possible and should write down these tentative decisions.

The development of tentative decisions or hypotheses as to what ought to happen is separate from actually making recommendations. At this stage the advocate is floating trial balloons, making suggestions and seeking other ideas or support for the position he or she is considering. Even a tentative identification of action is an important step in the process and is likely to move the matter into clearer definition of the problem and clearer identification of the possible solutions.

The degree of independent decision making on the part of the advocate will vary depending on the age of the child. An advocate who makes a decision contrary to a very young child's stated wishes should advise the young client of that position and should share the reasoning behind it. For example, if children say they wish to stay with parents who have been abusing or neglecting them, the child advocate must explain that until the court can be assured of their safety, the advocate cannot recommend that they remain with their parents without protective intervention. The child advocate also can reassure the children by informing them that the goal is to encourage the court to take steps to reunite the family.

Problem Solving and Mediation

A primary objective of child advocacy is to reduce adversarial relations among the parties that may prolong court involvement or negatively affect the child's well-being. In fact, the child advocate frequently functions as a mediator between conflicting parties to facilitate the resolution of problems and to foster positive steps toward strengthening and uniting families.

One mediation strategy is to identify the common ground among parties. Antagonism can be reduced by highlighting the common goals shared by the parties. Next, differences in problem identification and intervention goals should be addressed by identifying the expressed needs and preferences of each party and encouraging all sides to negotiate their positions so that an acceptable agreement can be made on the best course of action. Total agreement may not always be achieved among parties, but the child advocate can assist the parties in reaching an acceptable compromise by generating several alternatives to solving the presenting problem(s).

In order to perform problem-solving and mediation tasks, child advocates should consider the following questions:

1. What is the common ground among parties?
2. Are they clearly identified?
3. How can the problems be addressed?
4. What can help to solve the identified problems? Are there family members or other people who could protect the child?
5. Have all resources and possible courses of action been identified?

In generating alternatives and identifying potential resources, the child advocate should be sure to look beyond the traditional child welfare system—for example, to community-based nonprofit services, the family's informal social network, and church-based services consistent with the family's culture.

Much of the problem solving and negotiation around a case commonly takes place between court hearings. Therefore, the child advocate should maintain constant communication with all parties, so that information can be exchanged and problems can be worked through in a collaborative manner.

Identifying Action Steps

The child advocate should carefully identify a specific plan of action to represent the best interests of the child client. After coming to a tentative position on behalf of the child, considering it carefully, and perhaps discussing it with others, the advocate should decide on a position and write down action steps necessary to achieve the desired outcome. The action plan must be clear, but it also should allow for some flexibility to accommodate to changes in circumstances and the availability of new information. The child advocate may seek consultation from a supervising lawyer or others who are available to assist in developing a plan of action that specifies long-term and short-term goals. The key is discipline and organization.

Action steps can be of two sorts: in court and out of court. The advocate will certainly make a recommendation to the judge or referee. Out-of-court action, however, is an important element of child advocacy, one often overlooked in practice. The advocate should identify the plan for the child and family as to what is to happen from one court hearing to the next. Who will do what and when? The advocate does not have to develop the case plan, but one should be developed by the cadre of professionals at the hearing, and all participants should clearly understand the plan. That plan provides the basis for the final dimension of advocacy, follow-up.

Follow-up

The follow-up steps are critical. The child advocate spends a great amount of time nudging the system, by checking with various agencies and people to see that agreed-upon steps or court-appointed tasks are accomplished in an accurate and timely fashion. Advocates may often seem like unrelenting nags who fail to appreciate the limitations courts and social agencies face, but their follow-up is key. Many children fail to receive the services the court ordered, or such services are provided late. Such children may get lost in the system.

Follow-up activities usually involve extensive telephone work to remind, encourage, support, and in some cases assist parties with taking necessary actions and completing tasks. Follow-up also can be accomplished in face-to-face meetings with families, friends, professionals, or institutions associated with the case (among them neighbors, probation officers, family counselors and therapists, and schools) and by reading case files. Once an intervention plan has been approved, the child advocate can review and monitor the plan to ensure that it is carried out properly and efficiently. The advocate needs to be careful that he or she does not end up doing the job of the other professionals. It is not the advocate's job to arrange medical exams, psychological counseling, or other elements of the case plan, for example. It is the advocate's job to see that the elements of the case plan are implemented in a timely fashion. The advocate should be the squeaky wheel, albeit a polite one, for the client.

II
A Step-by-Step Guide through the Child Protection Process

The ten dimensions of advocacy discussed in chapter 6 can organize a child advocate's efforts at each stage of the court proceedings. This part presents a case example and follows it through five stages of the court process—preliminary hearing, pretrial conference, trial, dispositional hearing, and review hearings—analyzing the steps of the advocate at each procedural stage in terms of the ten dimensions. We will present another case example to analyze the advocate's role at the permanency planning hearing.

Case examples developed with special assistance from Roger Lauer.

7
Preliminary Hearing

The Legal Context

The first court hearing in the child protection process has different names in the various states, but the functions are essentially the same. Consistent with the practice in many states, we have called this first court hearing the preliminary hearing. The judge or referee must advise parents of their rights and will hear testimony and recommendations from all parties, including the child's advocate. The court must decide:

1. Whether there is probable cause to believe that the facts alleged are true.
2. Whether those facts, if true, constitute child neglect under state statutes.
3. Whether to authorize further court action by filing the petition.
4. Whether reasonable efforts have been made to prevent or eliminate the need for placement.
5. Whether a temporary placement should be made.

Despite the critical importance of the decisions regarding authorization of the petition and placement of the child, courts typically allot little time for preliminary hearings—frequently no more than twenty or thirty minutes. Consequently the courtroom affords little time for fact development, negotiation, or mediation. Therefore, the most important actions may be those taken before actually entering the courtroom. (See figure 7–1.)

Figure 7–1. Dimensions of Child Advocacy in the Child Protection Legal Process: Preliminary Hearing

PRELIMINARY HEARING	Pretrial Conference	Trial	Dispositional Hearing	Review Hearings	Permanency Planning Hearing

DIMENSIONS
Investigation
Consultation
Assessment
Identifying the child's interests
Permanency planning
Client counseling
Decision making
Problem solving
Identifying action steps
Follow-up

The Dimensions

Investigation and Fact Finding

Fact gathering is one of the most important functions in the preliminary hearing phase. What did someone see, hear, smell, taste, or feel to make him or her think that a particular child is abused or neglected? Who saw what, when, where?

When the child advocate first arrives at the court for the hearing, he or she should:

Obtain a copy of the petition and read it carefully.

Interview the social worker.

Speak with the child.

Speak with other principals as necessary and prioritized for the time available (for example police officers, medical personnel, neighbors, and relatives).

In the case we develop, we were assigned to represent seven-year-old Timmy Hunt.[1] We arrived at the court in advance of the scheduled preliminary hearing and began our work.

- What harm has the child suffered? What happened? where? when? how? by whom? How serious is the harm suffered? Does the child remain at risk? What are the options for protecting the child from further harm?
- What is the family compostion?
- What is the family's immediate home environment like?
- What are the parents like? What are their strengths? weaknesses? personal history of abuse or neglect? substance abuse or psychiatric problems?
- What is the child like? Is his or her social-psychological development normal for his or her age? How does the child do in school? Does he or she have special needs?
- Has the child contributed to the abuse or neglect? If so, how?

First, the child advocate read the petition and attached report. The petition filed by the protective services worker indicated that Timmy was a seven-year-old child who had been neglected and possibly abused by his mother. According to the petition and attached report, Ms. Hunt had placed Timmy on an airplane in California and sent him to his paternal aunt, who lived in a small town in Michigan. Two days earlier, Ms. Hunt had called the aunt and simply told her which plane Timmy would be on without offering her any chance to refuse. The mother indicated to the aunt that she could no longer handle the boy. The petition was filed by protective services because Timmy arrived without any of his medical records and therefore could not be enrolled in school or receive medical treatment.

The petition and attached report alleged that Timmy reacted with fear at the mention of returning to his mother. To his aunt and to the social worker, Timmy alluded to being hit with a board and being locked somewhere for long periods of time. He said that there was drug paraphernalia around the home. Timmy's father, the aunt's brother, was not married to his mother and reportedly lived in New Mexico.

The advocate for Timmy spoke with the child protective services social worker first. She told them that the mother seemed to have abandoned Timmy; attempts to locate her in the past several days had been unsuccessful. The worker had tried contacting the mother at her home address and other locations in two other states, with no success. Based on comments by the aunt, the worker thought that Ms. Hunt was traveling somewhere in the Northwest, with her boyfriend who had a long-distance trucking business. The worker reported that there was a question of whether Timmy's father, his aunt's brother, had ever admitted paternity.

The aunt was interviewed next. She is married with three children of her own, ages four, nine, and eleven. Her husband works days, and she sometimes works nights, but they live close to her husband's mother, who helps with child care.

The aunt retold the story of Timmy's arrival and went on to expand upon the child's "hysterical" reaction to his mother when she had phoned. Apparently Ms. Hunt had phoned twice to speak with Timmy, but he had refused to talk to her both times. The aunt stated that Timmy had frequent nightmares and had wet the bed a few times.

The aunt was asked about her brother. He has an alcohol problem, she said, and would not be fit to provide adequate parenting for Timmy. Ms. Hunt had tried to reach Timmy's father before contacting the aunt but had not been successful. The aunt confirmed that Timmy's father and mother had never been married. She did not know if paternity had ever been legally established.

Had she been present, the advocate would have spoken next with the mother —with her lawyer's permission if she had one. In her absence, the advocate moved directly to speak with Timmy.

Consultation

In consultation, the advocate seeks out the opinions and attitudes of the other major participants in the process—the social worker, police officers, parents or caretakers, the child, and others with knowledge, information, and insight. The goal of consultation is to gather views and perspectives as to what should happen to the child and family under the circumstances. Consultation gives meaning to facts, helps the advocate clarify the presenting problems, and provides possible solutions to those problems. At the preliminary hearing, consultation usually occurs simultaneously with investigation and fact finding.

- What does the social worker think the major problems are at this point? What does the social worker think should happen?
- Are other family members involved? What do they think should happen?
- What does the child think the major problems are at this point? What does he or she think should happen?
- What do the parents think the major problems are at this point? What do they think should happen?
- What do other professionals involved think the major problems are? What do they think should happen?

The social worker was concerned about Ms. Hunt's apparent abandonment of Timmy and his vague stories of physical abuse. She felt she needed additional information. In the meantime placement with his aunt should continue.

Timmy's aunt shared the concerns of the social worker but also wanted to clear up any barriers to getting him in school. Although concerned about Timmy, she was quite careful not to be critical of Ms. Hunt. She said she wanted to be helpful to the family but protective of the boy.

When asked what he thought the problems were, Timmy was not very communicative. He said simply that he wished to stay with his aunt.

Assessment

Building upon the factual information and preliminary opinions of others, the advocate should find out whether an accurate understanding of the family and its problems exists. Before a problem situation can be remedied, it must be carefully identified. Except in emergencies, the social worker should have a good preliminary assessment and a reasonable plan for intervention. What are the remaining questions? Is other information or expert evaluation required? As is the case in other stages of advocacy, the advocate should identify the needed action, identify who will take that action, tell others that he or she will follow up, and then follow up by telephone or in person.

- Does the social worker's assessment seem to be accurate?
- What is the relationship between the child and parents?
- What other assessment or professional evaluation is needed?
- Who will do what, by when?
- Identify follow up steps.

The advocate had unanswered questions and concerns after his first contacts. He decided to request an investigation to determine if Timmy's father had ever established paternity, so that the aunt would be a legal placement for him. He decided that a medical examination was necessary for purposes of getting Timmy properly admitted to school. Finally, and most important, he decided to request a psychological examination for Timmy to gain some insight into his behavior and to collect data about the abuse he may have suffered while living with his mother.

Identifying the Child's Interests

Protection from physical and emotional harm and provision of minimally adequate food, clothing, shelter, guidance, and supervision are certainly in the child's best interests. The social worker and the court generally address any obvious deficiencies in the child's care even without vigorous advocacy by an independent child advocate. But other interests are more subtle and may be overlooked by all but the child's representative.

- Is the child protected from physical and emotional harm?
- Is the child provided adequate food, clothing, shelter, guidance, and supervision?
- Have all reasonable efforts been made to protect the child in the home?
- If the child is placed outside the home, does the placement disrupt the child's life as little as possible?
- Is the placement in the least restrictive (most family-like) setting?
- Are regular and frequent visits with the parent(s) arranged?
- Is the case proceeding in a timely manner?
- Are necessary services being promptly provided to the child and family?

Timmy preferred to stay with his aunt where his basic needs were well cared for. He and his aunt wanted him to stay in the local school. Attempts to contact his mother and father were continuing. His aunt was willing for both parents to talk with him by telephone or visit him.

Permanency Planning

Even at the preliminary hearing, the advocate should keep an eye on the long-term consequences to the child of any placement. Perhaps the most critical decision in the child protection process is whether to make that first placement outside the child's home. The advocate should determine where the child's home is and whether that home is safe for the child. If it is not safe, the advocate must determine whether it can be made safe for the child and what reasonable efforts can be made to prevent or eliminate the need for placement. If a child needs to be placed, the advocate should try to identify a placement that is the least disruptive to the child's normal living arrangement. Can he or she be in a relative's or a friend's home. Can he or she be in the same neighborhood and in the same school? If a placement is necessary, the advocate needs an estimate as to how long the placement is likely to continue, keeping in mind the child's sense of time and the advantage, in most cases, of keeping placements as brief as possible.

- Is the child's home safe or can it be made safe pending further proceedings?
- What reasonable efforts can be made to prevent or eliminate the need for out-of-home placement?
- Are there people familiar to the child, such as relatives and friends or neighbors, who could care for him?

- What steps can be taken to see that the normal pattern of the child's life is disrupted as little as possible?
- How long is the placement likely to continue? Is the current placement available for as long as the child might need it?
- Has frequent visitation been arranged, or is there a compelling reason not to allow visits between parent and child?

The caseworker thought that the aunt's home was an excellent placement for Timmy. The advocate's impressions confirmed that opinion.

In response to the advocate's question, the aunt said that if Timmy's mother was unable to care for him, she was prepared to do so for the foreseeable future. Timmy said in the advocate's presence that he wanted to stay with his aunt.

Visitation with Ms. Hunt or the natural father was not possible since both were out of state. Telephone contact would be encouraged by the aunt.

Client Counseling

Children are often confused and uncertain as they are brought into the court process; they do not understand what is happening to them and their families. They may have preferences about where they go to live. They sometimes wish to stay with parents who have been abusing or neglecting them. The advocate can help by developing enough of a relationship with the youth to tell him or her what to expect of the court process and to explore with the child his or her preferences for a temporary home and services. At a level consistent with the maturity of the child, the advocate should discuss the various options presented by all parties to address the issues. The advocate must emphasize to the child that the final decision is the referee's or judge's and not the child's.

The counseling process can be complex. The advocate can do some explaining and try to clarify the child's wishes but should avoid serious psychological counseling.

- Does the child have questions about the court process?
- How does the child feel about the options presented by all parties to this point?
- What does the child want to see happen as a result of these proceedings?
- Where does the child want to live now?
- What other preferences does the child have about placement, visitation, school, and so on?
- What does the child want communicated to the court, social worker, or parent?

Timmy was interviewed with his aunt present. Because he was so young, it was hoped that he would eventually feel comfortable speaking with the advocate if his aunt were present for awhile. Despite the advocate's best efforts, he had to be coaxed by his aunt to say anything. Timmy said that he was told to forget about things that had frightened him from before (when he was living with his mother). Timmy was shy and would not speak directly with the advocate. His aunt attempted to intervene by rephrasing the questions for him, but to no avail.

Timmy did tell the advocate that he wanted to stay with his aunt "forever" and that he did not wish to live with his mother.

Decision Making and Coming to a Tentative Position

Having gathered information and consulted with the child, the social worker, parents, and others who may have knowledge of or an interest in the child's welfare, the advocate must make some decisions, though they may be tentative or preliminary. What position should the advocate take on behalf of the child? What are the goals for this particular procedural stage? What are the long-term goals that can be identified given the information available. The advocate should be as specific as possible, writing down the goals.

At this stage, the development of tentative positions or hypotheses as to what ought to happen should be separated from implementation of any recommendation. Now the advocate is floating trial balloons, making suggestions and seeking other ideas or support for the position he or she is considering. Even a tentative identification of action steps is an important step in the process and is likely to move the matter into clearer definition of the problem and clearer identification of the possible solutions to the problem.

- Should the court authorize or deny the filing of a petition or delay for a period of time?
- Where should the child be placed?
- What visitation should be arranged or ordered?
- Are additional medical or psychological exams necessary?
- What other matters can be dealt with at this hearing?

The advocate decided to recommend that the court authorize the petition and that Timmy be placed temporarily with his aunt as the protective services worker requested.

The aunt seemed quite committed to Timmy, but his placement with her would be legal only is she were a legal relative. The advocate was unsure whether legal paternity had ever been established. He thought it ought to be if it was not and decided to recommend that the court investigate the issue.

A medical and psychological exam seemed necessary for Timmy.

Problem Solving and Mediation

Having identified the problems as clearly as possible, the advocate may consider how they may be addressed. There are almost always some common interests among the parties. Identifying them. Avoid creating a strictly adversarial atmosphere. Instead, ask how the various parties can work together in the child's interests. The child probably has relationships with parents and other family members that should be preserved or nurtured. The advocate can consider how to promote a nonadversarial approach to resolving the problems presented by the family. If the parents cannot protect the child, are there other family members or other people known to the child who could?

The child advocate may play a significant role as mediator. He or she is neither the petitioner's attorney nor the defense attorney and need not take an adversarial position on either side. The interest of the child is often served by voluntary resolution of the legal dispute, thus avoiding contested trial. A contested proceeding will not only delay adoption of a treatment plan but put additional stresses on a family, perhaps delaying the child's return home. The child's advocate therefore may be a useful mediator and may assume responsibility for finding terms of settlement that all parties find acceptable. There's an old bromide among attorneys: "I've lost trials, but I've never lost a settlement."

The potential impact of other institutions and agencies beyond the traditional child welfare system need to be considered when fashioning a settlement agreement. Other courts, schools, employment, housing, and so forth can have a significant effect on an allegedly maltreated child and family. The other institutions can either make the problems for the child more difficult or provide help and support.

Research has shown that abusive and neglectful families identify concrete services such as housing and employment as being more helpful than "soft services" such as counseling.[2] Poverty is also a significant stressor in families experiencing child abuse and neglect.[3]

- What are the common interests among the parties?
- Can the advocate promote a cooperative resolution of any of these problems?
- Can other institutions and systems besides child welfare and the courts assist in addressing any problems?

The worker, the aunt, and Timmy agreed that he should stay with his aunt. There was a common view among all parties that there ought to continue to be free communication with Ms. Hunt should she call. The tone at this point was one of supportive concern for Timmy's welfare and hope that a cooperative resolution in his welfare would result.

Looking at other institutions, the advocate urged that the social worker ascertain whether in fact Timmy's father had ever formally acknowledged paternity, a question that would take her to the circuit or probate court records.

The protective services worker suggested a court-ordered and supervised guardianship in which Ms. Hunt agreed to Timmy's staying with his aunt as a way to resolve this case without further damage to the family relationships. The worker agreed to provide the necessary forms for the aunt in case the mother agreed with this resolution.

The community mental health system was a logical source of the psychological assistance the aunt need for Timmy. The advocate asked the social worker that it be pursued. Finally, Timmy needed a medical exam so he could be enrolled in school.

Identifying Action Steps

Having firmed up the goals, however tentative, for the child, the advocate must act to achieve them. He or she should suspend judgment until the facts are gathered and the case assessed; moreover, the course of action needs to be decided before specific steps are taken. In an actual case, these steps may be taken quite rapidly; tentative positions will be raised before action is really necessary. The linear step-by-step approach suggested here may help organized the advocate's thoughts and duties in an environment that can often be quite chaotic and confused.

Two sorts of action steps can be considered: in court and out of court. The advocate should decide on action steps and write them down. The advocate will take some action at the preliminary hearing itself. Out-of-court actions, however, are important pressure points for child advocates, one often overlooked in practice. The advocate should identify steps for the child and family as to what is expected to happen from one court hearing to the next. Who will do what, when? That plan will provide the basis for the final dimension of advocacy, follow-up.

- What needs to be done to protect the child?
- What action does the advocate want the court to take?
- What action should the social worker take?
- What action should others take?
- What should the advocate do? Who is to do what, when? What services does the family need? How will these services be provided? by whom? when?

Once in the courtroom, the advocate recommended that the court authorize the petition and that Timmy be placed temporarily with his aunt. He also asked that paternity be investigated and established if it had not been, so that Timmy's placement with his aunt would be clearly legal.

The advocate requested that a medical exam and psychological exam be ordered for Timmy.

After hearing the statements of the parties present, the judge entered the court order, authorizing the petition and placing Timmy with his aunt as recommended. A psychological exam and medical exam were ordered. The social worker agreed to check into paternity.

The court set a date for a pretrial conference in three weeks.

Follow-up

The often unglamorous follow-up is of critical importance. Advocates may often seem like unrelenting nags who fail to appreciate the limitations facing the courts and social agencies, but follow-up is key. Many children fail to receive the services the court ordered or services are provided late, and children get lost in the system. The advocate should not let it happen to children for whom he or she is responsible. Follow-up is usually done by telephone but can also include meetings with the child, family, friends, and professionals and reading case files. Before the principal parties have left the courthouse, the advocate must develop a clear and precise list of what is to happen, by when, and who is going to do it.

Having identified who is to do what and when, the advocate follows up to see that the steps are, in fact, taken. That psychological exam, for instance, is easy for the worker to agree to and critical for charting the direction of the case, but in the face of the many demands on social workers, it may not be arranged as soon as is desirable. The advocate must be the squeaky wheel, albeit a polite one, for the client.

- Identify steps to be taken by the advocate and others before the next court appearance.
- Contact principals either in person or by telephone to get the steps accomplished.
- Keep a tickler system of reminders of important follow-up steps.

Immediately upon leaving the courtroom, the advocate developed a list of tasks for follow-up. He identified who was to do what, by when. He decided to follow-up on the paternity questions, on the psychological and medical evaluation for Timmy; to visit the aunt's home to see where Timmy was living and what the home was like; and to investigate the quantity and quality of contact between Timmy and his mother since his arrival in Michigan.

After a court-ordered placement, the agency policy required that the case be reassigned to a foster care worker for additional reviews. The protective services worker would continue to come to court as petitioner, however, until the court granted or denied the petition.

Another goal of the advocate was to identify and begin to form a working relationship with the new foster care worker who now had responsibility for case services. He contacted the agency and found out which caseworker had been assigned to the case. He called the caseworker, introduced himself, and stressed the importance of a prompt psychological evaluation for Timmy and the usefulness of a medical exam.

The foster care worker informed the advocate that she had just received the case and would not have any time to contact Timmy's aunt for two weeks. She was unwilling to commit herself concerning either the evaluation or the exam until she had contacted the family. This presented some difficulty for the advocate since the pretrial conference was scheduled in three weeks. If the caseworker agreed with his recommendations, she would have only one week to schedule and carry out both the psychological and medical exams. Obviously there was not enough time for these exams, so the advocate decided to focus his attention on the home visit with the aunt's family.

The advocate called the aunt and arranged to meet her and Timmy at her home in preparation for the pretrial conference.

Notes

1. The case example is a composite of several actual cases. All names and other identifying information have been changed to protect confidentiality.

2. Kathleen C. Faller, ed., *Social Work with Abused and Neglected Children: A Manual of Interdisciplinary Practice* (New York: Free Press, 1981).

3. American Humane Association, *National Study of the Incidence of Child Abuse and Neglect* (Denver: The Association, 1981).

8
Pretrial Conference

The Legal Context

The pretrial conference is designed to clarify the issues to be addressed at trial, to limit the number of issues the court must address, if possible, and to ensure that the case is ready for trial. The conference is presided over by the judge, but generally there is opportunity for informal discussion among the parties prior to entering the courtroom. A pretrial conference also provides an opportunity to settle a case without formal trial. For the child advocate, the informal opportunities for resolving issues that affect the child are especially important. While the lawyers for the agency and the parent focus on legal details preliminary to bringing a matter to trial, the child advocate should center his or her attention on ways to further the interests of the child.

In Michigan, for example, a pretrial conference should:

1. Establish satisfactory proof of process (that is, have all persons who have a legal interest in the proceedings been given legal notice of the child maltreatment charges and the date and time of hearing?).

2. Establish proper parties (that is, those with a legal interest in the child and these proceedings; generally proper parties include parents and legal guardians, the child, and the state).

3. Review the status of the file to ensure there are no outstanding reports or orders necessary to resolution of the issues.

4. Clarify the procedural status of the proceedings.

5. Determine the placement of the children and ensure their continued protection pending trial.

6. Clarify the contents of the petition and delete or amend the petition as necessary.

7. Establish the nature of the parental conduct and the juvenile code section allegedly violated.

8. Disclose the nature of the defense (for example, denial or mistaken identity).

9. Identify legal contentions, if any, and fix the deadline for submitting written legal arguments to the court.

10. Arrange for further psychological or medical evaluations by stipulation (that is, agreement of the parties) or court order.

11. Determine the number of witnesses.

12. Identify expert witnesses; stipulate to qualifications and testimony as much as possible.

13. Identify proposed exhibits and admit as to authenticity where possible.

14. Set the trial date.

15. Estimate how long the trial will last.

16. Discuss settlement possibilities.

Of most interest to the child advocate is the opportunity to seek settlement of the matter promptly and without a full adversarial contest. The matter could be dismissed, or the respondent (parent) could enter a plea to the petition as it stands or as amended, thereby accepting formal court jurisdiction over the child. Some other negotiated settlement could be reached, with possibilities limited only by the facts of the case and the imagination of the participants. Generally all parties and their attorneys are present at the court, including the children if old enough. Their presence allows the attorneys to confer with them and negotiate settlement or agreements with full information from the clients and with their consultation and approval. The informal discussions at this stage can be significant to a case resolution and to the future welfare of the child. Subsequent to informal discussions, all parties typically enter a courtroom and tell the court on the record what has been acccomplished.

The first few weeks of a case are extremely critical for the future of the child. The true nature of the problem must be discerned and responses likely to address the problem identified and put into place. The independent, persistent, and aggressive attention of the advocate at this stage can pay great dividends as the case evolves. (See figure 8–1.)

The Dimensions

Investigation and Fact Finding

Although fact gathering is an ongoing process in child protection, it is most critical at the early phases of preliminary hearing and pretrial conference. A fairly accurate factual picture of the child and his or her situation ought to be available to the court at the time of trial. Although additional insight into the nature of the

Figure 8-1. Dimensions of Child Advocacy
in the Child Protection Legal Process: Pretrial Conference

Preliminary Hearing	**PRETIAL CONFERENCE**	Trial	Dispositional Hearing	Review Hearings	Permanency Planning Hearing

DIMENSIONS

Investigation
Consultation
Assessment
Identifying the child's interests
Permanency planning
Client counseling
Decision making
Problem solving
Identifying action steps
Follow-up

harm suffered by the child or the strengths and weaknesses of the family is likely to come up at almost any time, one of the principal purposes of the early stages of the court process is to ascertain the facts.

- Have there been any significant new developments since the last hearing?

Follow-up on questions from preliminary hearing:

- What harm has the child suffered? What happened? Where? When? How? By whom? How serious is the harm suffered? Does the child remain at risk?
- What are the options for protecting the child from further harm?
- What is the family like?
- What is the family and child's immediate home environment like?
- What are the parents like? What are their strengths and weaknesses? Is there a personal history of abuse or neglect? of substance or psychiatric problems?
- What is the child like?

The advocate contacted Timmy's aunt to arrange a visit to her home. Over the telephone she informed them that Timmy's mother had called and spoken to the aunt's husband. The protective services worker had given the aunt and uncle the necessary guardianship papers, so the aunt's husband asked the mother for an address to send them to for the mother's signature. Ms. Hunt told the aunt to send the papers with her brother who lived in the area and planned to meet her in Cleveland the next week. She also asked the aunt to send Timmy with her brother so she could visit with him in Cleveland. The aunt was unsure of what to do about the request to send Timmy to Ohio.

Several days after the telephone call, the advocate visited Timmy at his aunt's home. Ms. Hunt had called again the previous weekend and threatened to come and take Timmy. Timmy at first refused to speak with his mother but, after encouragement from his aunt, did speak with her. Timmy told his mother that he did not want to leave.

The aunt said that Timmy had become very aggressive and violent with her own children. He had tried to convince her youngest son to drink bleach and on another occasion attempted to push him down a flight of stairs. On both occasions Timmy had told his aunt, "I don't want him [her son] here!" The aunt had become so concerned that she tried to arrange a psychological examination on her own. She was told by the local community mental health program that there was a three-month waiting list for an appointment.

At this interview the aunt was quite frustrated with Timmy and the whole situation and she began to express doubts about whether she could handle him in her home. She suggested that Timmy might need to be placed in an environment where he could receive a lot of individual attention.

After some discussion, she felt that Timmy could remain with her only if she had some idea about his psychological status and could receive some instruction in behavioral management.

The advocate asked whether the foster care worker had contacted her about a psychological evaluation. She said the worker had contacted her by telephone but had not mentioned an examination.

The advocate spoke briefly with Timmy alone and was struck by the extent of his violent and aggressive talk. In addition Timmy described his mother's beating him with a stick on his rear and slapping him across the face.

When Timmy's father was contacted in New Mexico by the protective service worker he said he had formally acknowledged paternity in a nearby county. The worked obtained the necessary documentation. Paternity, and thus the relationship with the aunt, was established. Timmy could legally remain in his home under juvenile court order.

Consultation

As at other phases of the court process, the advocate needs to gather not only the facts but also opinions, viewpoints, and suggestions for resolution of the family problems. Generally all points of view should be carefully elicited and considered.

- What do the social worker and other professionals involved in the case think the major problems are? What do they think should happen?
- What do the parents and other family members think the major problems are? What do they think should happen?
- What do the advocate's supervising professionals think the major problems are? What do they think should happen?

After consulting with his supervising attorney, the advocate informed the aunt that Timmy could not leave the state without the permission of the court.

At the pretrial conference itself, the advocate again consulted with the aunt, who reaffirmed her desire to keep Timmy with her family and sought to "retract" the expression of frustration she had made during the earlier home visit. She had contacted a private psychologist on her own about Timmy's behavior and about her reaction to him and in a few telephone conversations was able to understand why Timmy was acting so aggressively.

The protective service worker's attitude was unchanged from the preliminary hearing. She felt Timmy was in some danger in his mother's custody, that she had essentially abandoned him, and that Timmy's best interests were served by his remaining with his aunt.

Ms. Hunt appeared with her lawyer and her brother. The advocate consulted with her, with her lawyer present. At first the lawyer misinterpreted the advocate's role. Mistaking him for the prosecutor, the attorney denied any wrongdoing by his client and offered to have her submit to a lie detector test.

The advocate explained that his role was to represent Timmy's best interests and referred the lawyer to the prosecutor for those issues. Ms. Hunt told the advocate her version of events: that she had Timmy sent to his aunt because she and her boyfriend were travelling a great deal because of some new business opportunities. She claimed that the aunt understood this was only supposed to be temporary and was trying to "steal" Timmy. When asked about their relationship, Ms. Hunt said that she and Timmy were not close. She agreed that Timmy did not have anybody whom he considered to be his father. She said Timmy was hyperactive and that she spanked him only to discipline him but nothing more. She told the advocate that she wanted to take Timmy back to California with her to be evaluated by a psychologist there; however, she indicated that she would get the evaluation in Michigan because people seemed to think it was needed. She claimed that Timmy had been abused at one time long ago, but that was by his biological father, who also abused her.

Ms. Hunt had the guardianship papers but was unwilling to sign them. She wanted to wait and think about it and see what developed.

The advocate spoke with the mother's brother, who supported his sister but wanted Timmy to live with him if he was not returned to her custody. He was a divorced father of two, unemployed, and living alone in a nearby town. He thought he would have no problems getting Tim enrolled in school or evaluated by a psychologist.

Assessment

- Does the court have sufficient information and professional advice about the child, the family, and the presenting problems?
- What other assessment or professional evaluation is needed?
- Who will do what, when?

At the time of the pretrial conference, Timmy's psychological exam still had not been arranged. His medical exam had been completed by the aunt's family physician, and he was found to be physically normal and healthy.

Identifying the Child's Interests

- Is the child protected from physical and emotional harm?
- Is the child provided adequate food, clothing, shelter, guidance, and supervision?
- Have all reasonable efforts been made to protect child in his home?
- If the child is placed, does the placement disrupt the child's life as little as possible?
- Is the placement in the least restrictive (most family-like setting)?
- Are regular and frequent visits with the parent(s) arranged?
- Is the case proceeding in a timely manner?
- Are necessary services being promptly provided to the child and family?

Timmy was physically safe with his aunt, and all his daily needs were being met. He was now enrolled in school. By this time, after the passage of several weeks, the aunt's home was the place to which Timmy was accustomed and had the further advantage of being a family-like setting in the home of a relative.

There had been no delays in the court proceeding, and none were anticipated.

Although Timmy did not want to live with his mother, the advocate decided that visits between them were quite important to maintain or restore whatever relationship they had.

Permanency Planning

- Is the child's home safe, or can it be made safe, pending further proceedings?
- What reasonable efforts can be made to prevent or eliminate the need for out-of-home placement?
- Are there people familiar to the child, such as relatives and friends or neighbors, who could care for him or her?
- What steps can be taken to see that the normal pattern of the child's life is disrupted as little as possible?
- How long is the placement likely to continue? Is the current placement available for as long as the child might need to be in placement?
- Has frequent visitation been arranged, or is there compelling reason not to allow visits between parent and child?

At this point, it seemed that Ms. Hunt had no settled home, even if there were no outstanding questions of Timmy's safety. There were no reasonable efforts that could be taken to eliminate the need for placement.

Should a permanent home away from Ms. Hunt be required, the aunt, despite some wavering during the advocate's visit, now reasserted her willingness to keep Timmy for as long as necessary.

Visits to maintain the connection, the "bridge," between Ms. Hunt and Timmy were encouraged by the advocate.

Client Counseling

- Does the child have questions about the court process?
- How does the child feel about the options presented by all parties to this point?
- What does the child want to see happen as a result of these proceedings?
- Where does the child want to live now?
- What other preferences does the child have about placement, visitation, school and so on?
- What does the child want communicated to the court, social worker, or parent(s)?
- Emphasize that the final decision is the judge's, not the child's.

Timmy had become more comfortable with the advocate by now as a known and trusted person. He reaffirmed that he did not want to return to his mother but wanted to stay with his aunt forever. When asked about his biological father, Timmy did not know who he was.

He told the advocate clearly, once again, that he was frightened by his mother and did not want to live with her. He liked living with his aunt and wished to stay there. It was all right with him to visit his mother but not to live with her.

The advocate explained that the judge would hear about his situation and would be the one to decide where Timmy would live but that the advocate would tell the judge what Timmy had told him. Timmy was satisfied with what the advocate proposed to do.

Decision Making and Coming to a Tentative Position

- What should the advocate be prepared to recommend to the court about setting the matter for trial?
- Is a plea possible at this time?
- Will adjournment of the pretrial conference serve any useful settlement purpose? That is, are there steps that, if accomplished in the next few weeks, could eliminate the need for court jurisdiction or permit the parents to accept jurisdiction without trial?
- Where should the child be placed pending trial?
- What visitation should be arranged or ordered?
- Are additional medical or psychological exams required?

The advocate decided that Timmy's interests would be best served by setting the matter for trial so that the questions about whether Ms. Hunt provided proper care for Timmy could be resolved. It did not seem that Ms. Hunt was particularly conciliatory or that delaying the formal proceedings would work in any way to Timmy's advantage. Besides, the judge was known to be concerned that cases regarding children be promptly resolved. Only upon a showing of particular need would he delay a case.

Pending consultation with the other parties, the advocate decided to recommend continued placement with the aunt, visitation between Ms. Hunt and Timmy, and that elusive psychological exam.

Problem Solving and Mediation

- What are the common interests among the parties?
- Can the advocate promote a cooperative resolution of any of the problems?

- Can any other institutions besides child welfare and the courts assist in addressing any problems?

The advocate tried to lay the seeds for an agreement among the parties; however, the various sides could not resolve their differences. The advocate reviewed the possible solutions that existed for Timmy and concluded that although he favored continued placement with Timmy's aunt, a foster care placement in the local area might help ease some of the tensions between Ms. Hunt and the aunt and promote settlement—if Timmy could accept such an alternative. Return to the mother's custody in the short term seemed unacceptable. But the foster care option did not help promote a settlement at this time. Ms. Hunt's attorney was still pressing for Timmy's return to his mother. Ms. Hunt preferred that Timmy stay with the aunt he knew rather than a stranger. A foster care placement was inconsistent with Timmy's interest in continuity and stability anywhere. The advocate did not need to pursue the idea of foster care any further.

Identifying Action Steps

- What needs to be done to protect the child?
- What action does the advocate want the court to take?
- What action should the social worker take?
- What action should others take?
- Who is to do what, when? What services does the family need? How will these services be provided? by whom? when?

When the parties entered the courtroom for the pretrial conference before the judge, the advocate recommended that placement be continued with the aunt and that an immediate psychological evaluation be carried out for Timmy. The advocate stated to the court that he believed Timmy was afraid of his mother and did not want to return to her home. In addition, he liked living with his aunt and wanted to stay with her. Finally the advocate told the judge of Timmy's statements regarding physical abuse by his mother, which probably should be investigated further.

Ms. Hunt's lawyer reiterated her claim that Timmy's biological father was responsible for any abuse that had occurred and that Timmy had been sent to the aunt for a short-term prearranged visit. The lawyer also argued that the Michigan court lacked jurisdiction to rule on the custody of Timmy since neither the boy nor his parents was a resident of the state.

The court ruled that it had proper jurisdiction because the boy was physically found within the county and set the matter for trial. On the issues affecting Timmy's welfare in the interim, the judge concurred with the advocate's recommendations. Besides continuing placement with the aunt, the judge told the foster care worker to set up a psychological evaluation immediately for Timmy. With a direct order from the judge, the court was able to bypass the three-month waiting period for the exam that the aunt had encountered.

The mother's lawyer requested visitation privileges. The aunt was quite willing to accomodate Ms. Hunt and was eager to keep as much harmony as possible within the family. The advocate agreed with visitation, as did the social worker and prosecutor. The judge granted visitation at the convenience of the aunt and only in her home. A trial date was set for two weeks.

Follow-up

- Identify steps to be taken by advocate and others before the next court appearance.
- Contact principals either in person or by telephone to get the steps accomplished.
- Keep a tickler system of reminders of important follow-up steps.

After leaving the courtroom, the advocate developed a list of tasks to follow-up. Most important, he decided to remain in contact with the social worker to ensure that Timmy's psychological exam was carried out. In addition, he checked with the social worker about forwarding a copy of the report once it was received.

The advocate called the aunt to check on her relationship with Timmy and his visits with his mother. He attempted to arrange a time to observe a visit but was not able to do so.

Finally, the advocate tried to contact Ms. Hunt to arrange an interview and observation of her brother's home but was unsuccessful because there was no telephone in the home.

9
Trial

The Legal Context

The advocate can play a significant role before the case is called for trial, but when the case finally gets before the trial judge, the responsibilities of the child advocate are limited. At trial the major issues are technical, legal ones. Are the facts, as alleged in by the petition, true? Do those facts constitute legal neglect as defined by the state statutes? The procedural steps up to this point are intended to prepare for a full and fair presentation of the case to the judge (or a jury in some states), with the parents given a chance to counter the allegations against them.

The question before the court is whether the youngster is an abused or neglected child as defined by the state's statute. Under the circumstances of this case, does the state have a right to interfere with the privacy and freedom of these parents and this child? The state has the authority to interfere in private family life only if the petitioner proves that the facts alleged in the petition are true and that those facts constitute legal neglect according to the state's laws.

The attorney with whom the advocate is working will have responsibility for identifying witnesses who should be called in the child's interests. The advocate is charged with independently representing the child. He or she may act completely independently or may decide that collaboration with one side or another will further the child's interests. Where the child advocate has decided to support the petitioner's case, the advocate's attorney will also consult with the agency lawyer to be sure the proper witnesses will be called to prove that the child is abused or neglected. In some cases, the child advocate may disagree with the social agency and may side with the parents. Then the child advocate's attorney will work with the parents' lawyer in preparation for trial.

Settlement of these matters short of trial is generally a priority for the child advocate. Mediation and problem solving become predominant dimensions of advocacy for the child advocate at the trial stage. (See figure 9–1.)

Figure 9–1. Dimensions of Child Advocacy
in the Child Protection Legal Process: Trial

Preliminary Hearing	Pretrial Conference	**TRIAL**	Dispositional Hearing	Review Hearings	Permanency Planning Hearing

DIMENSIONS

Investigation
Consultation
Assessment
Identifying the child's interests
Permanency planning
Client counseling
Decision making
Problem solving
Identifying action steps
Follow-up

The Dimensions

Investigation and Fact Finding

Most of the facts of the case should be well known by trial. In child abuse and neglect cases, however, new factual developments often come to the light as late as the day of trial itself. The advocate should be alert to such developments and relevant questions. Important new developments, including changes of heart by parents and social workers alike, provide opportunities for settling the case and addressing the family problems.

- Have any new developments occurred since the last hearing?

Prior to the scheduled trial, the advocate received a copy of the long-awaited psychological evaluation of Timmy. The psychological assessment cast significant light on the family situation and opened up opportunities to resolve the matter.

Consultation

Consultation at the trial stage generally is in the context of seeking some resolution of the question of formal court jurisdiction. Suggestions for resolution of the family problems may come from many quarters. Generally all points of view should be carefully elicited and considered.

- What do the social worker, and other professionals involved in the case think the major problems are? What do they think should happen?
- What do the parents and other family members think the major problems are? What do they think should happen?
- What do the advocate's supervising professionals think the major problems are? What do they think should happen?

The positions of the social worker and agency attorney remained the same: Timmy should live with his aunt, with visits by his mother, until such time as the mother's living situation could be adequately evaluated. To get an adequate evaluation, court jurisdiction seemed necessary. Ms. Hunt's position was also unchanged: she was not guilty of child neglect and wanted Timmy back in her care.

Assessment

- Does the court have sufficient information and professional advice about the child, the family, and the presenting problems?
- What other assessment or professional evaluation is needed?
- Who will do what, when?

The psychologist had found that Timmy showed little bonding with his mother. Further, Timmy made comments to the psychologist that his mother had physically abused him, as had her boyfriend.

The evaluation also showed that Timmy had formed a strong attachment to his aunt and her family. His ability to form the attachment was attributed to a prior close relationship he had had with his maternal grandparents at age two.

The psychologist recommended that Timmy not be removed from his aunt's care until more was known about the mother's suitability as a parent.

Identifying the Child's Interests

- Is the child protected from physical and emotional harm?
- Is the child provided adequate food, clothing, shelter, guidance, and supervision?
- Have all reasonable efforts been made to protect the child in the home?
- If the child is placed, does the placement disrupt the child's life as little as possible?
- Is the placement in the least restrictive (most family like) setting?

- Are regular and frequent visits with the parent(s) arranged?
- Is the case proceeding in a timely manner?
- Are necessary services being promptly provided to the chid and family?

Timmy remained physically safe with his aunt, and all his daily needs were being met. Several visits had occurred between Timmy and Ms. Hunt, and they neither caused additional harm to Timmy, nor did they cause him to change his mind about not wanting to live with his mother.

Ms. Hunt was currently in transit from California and planned to settle in Ohio. She had no established home at this time to which Timmy could return.

Timmy's established custodial environment had become his aunt's home.

Permanency Planning

- Is the child's home safe (or can it be made safe) pending further proceedings?
- What reasonable efforts can be made to prevent or eliminate the need for out-of-home placement?
- Are there people familiar to the child, such as relatives and friends or neighbors, who could care for him or her?
- What steps can be taken to disrupt the normal pattern of the child's life as little as possible?
- How long is the placement likely to continue? Is the current placement available for as long as the child might need to be in placement?
- Has frequent visitation been arranged, or is there compelling reason not to allow visits between parent and child?

Ms. Hunt still had no settled home. There were no reasonable efforts that could be taken to eliminate the need for placement. Timmy's aunt remained willing to keep Timmy for as long as necessary but was also willing to allow frequent visits between him and Ms. Hunt.

Client Counseling

- Does the child have questions about the court process?
- How does the child feel about the options presented by all parties to this point?

- What does the child want to see happen as a result of these proceedings?
- Where does the child want to live now?
- What other preferences does the child have about placement, visitation, school, and so forth?
- What does the child want communicated to the court, social worker, or parent?
- Emphasize that the final decision is the judge's and not the child's.

Timmy continued to say that he did not want to return to his mother but wanted to stay with his aunt. He understood that the judge would hear about his situation and would decide what was to happen.

Decision Making and Coming to a Tentative Position

- What should the advocate be prepared to recommend to the court?
- Is a plea possible at this time?
- What are the goals of the advocate at this time?

After consultation with the supervising attorney, the advocate decided that Timmy's interests would be best served by following the recommendation of the psychologist—that Timmy continue living with his aunt until a psychological exam of Ms. Hunt could be obtained to help learn more about her suitability as a parent and her relationship with Timmy.

The advocate hoped that eventually Timmy could return to his mother and wanted to encourage their relationship. Most immediately, however, the advocate had determined that continued placement with the aunt was best for Timmy.

There were at least two ways to achieve continued placement with the aunt: 1) juvenile court jurisdiction based on the mother's neglect and (2) guardianship in the aunt ordered through the court if Ms. Hunt voluntarily consented.

Problem Solving and Mediation

- What are the common interests among the parties?
- Can the advocate promote a cooperative resolution of any of these problems?
- What other institutions besides child welfare and the court can assist in addressing any problems?

As the parties were gathering for the trial, Ms. Hunt's attorney, having read the psychologist's report approached the child advocate with an offer to bargain.

He asked whether the advocate would agree to adjourning the trial so Ms. Hunt could be psychologically evaluated. If the results of the exam confirmed the abuse charge, she would enter a plea to the petition.

The advocate thought that avoiding trial would probably be in Timmy's interest but that a timely resolution issue was also important. Based on consultation with the supervising attorney, he thought that the legal case was quite strong and that the petition could be proved at the trial. He rejected the mother's attorney's offer but stressed how much he hoped that Timmy and his mother could eventually be reunited. The advocate asked whether Ms. Hunt wanted Timmy to live with her. What was her attitude about Timmy's continuing to live with his aunt based on juvenile court jurisdiction or guardianship?

Ms. Hunt's attorney never responded to the guardianship option but, after talking further with his client, he quickly made another offer based on juvenile court authority. First, he wanted assurances that the child advocate was sincere in wanting to see Timmy reunited with his mother if her home could be shown to be safe for him. The advocate gave those assurances.

The advocate, obliged to represent Timmy's point of view, felt in a real bind.

Timmy, aged seven, had made it repeatedly clear that he did not want to return to his mother's custody. The advocate's peronal adult sense was that a sincere effort to reunite mother and son was called for and was in Timmy's long-range best interests. He knew the policy of the social agency and the court, is to reunite families whenever possible and the law presumes parents fit to care for their children. And he hoped that Timmy, after counseling, would want to return to his mother's care. The advocate believed that he would privately urge Timmy to return to his mother's custody if counseling were successful. All in all, the advocate took a bit of a risk in giving these assurances, knowing that if Timmy refused to accept return to his mother's custody, the advocate would strongly present Timmy's point of view to the agency and the court.

Hunt's attorney then offered to have Ms. Hunt plead no contest to child neglect and submit to a psychological exam in advance of the dispositional hearing—but under certain conditions. He would recommend this course to her if he could be assured that strong consideration would be given to returning Timmy to his mother, perhaps after a period of counseling, should the psychological exam reveal no serious obstacles. Ms. Hunt said she was willing to stay in the local area for as long as it took to settle matters for Timmy. She said she really wanted to have him back in her care.

The child advocate agreed. The matter was discussed with the social worker and the prosecuting attorney, and the aunt was consulted. All agreed to this resolution.

Identifying Action Steps

- **What needs to be done to protect the child?**

- What action does the advocate want the court to take?
- What action should the social worker take?
- What action should others take?
- Who is to do what, when? What services does the family need? How will these services be provided? by whom? when?

All parties entered the courtroom. The prosecuting attorney addressed the judge and recited the agreement to enter a no-contest plea to an amended petition that alleged neglect only. The prosecutor asked that a psychological evaluation of Ms. Hunt be scheduled as soon as possible, to be completed before a dispositional hearing four weeks later. The prosecutor expressed the wish that all parties find a way to work with Ms. Hunt so that Timmy could eventually be returned to her custody.

The judge asked each party in turn if he or she agreed to such a resolution. After each party agreed, the judge formally took a no-contest plea from Ms. Hunt.

The court formally assumed jurisdiction over Timmy Hunt, ordered further investigation by the social worker, including a psychological exam of Ms. Hunt, ordered continued visitation, and set the matter for dispositional hearing in four weeks.

Follow-up

- Identify steps to be taken by the advocate and others before the next court appearance.
- Contact principals either in person or by telephone to get the steps accomplished.
- Keep a tickler system of reminders of important follow-up steps.

The advocate's list of steps to be taken included arranging the psychological exam (social worker's and Ms. Hunt's responsibility); monitoring visits (social worker's responsibility); and preparing a recommendation for the dispositional hearing (social worker's responsibility, although the advocate needed to come to his own independent recommendation).

10
Disposition

The Legal Context

Although the question of what protection and what services ought to be provided to the child is of central importance for the child advocate from the very beginning of the process, the court, after entering limited and necessary emergency orders, does not reach it as a formal matter until the dispositional hearing. (See figure 10–1) At this point, the court has determined that it has the power to suspend the privacy interests of the parents and the child and intervene in the family life for the protection of the child and possible rehabilitation of the family unit.

**Figure 10-1. Dimensions of Child Advocacy
in the Child Protection Legal Process: Disposition**

Preliminary Hearing	Pretrial Conference	Trial	DISPOSITIONAL HEARING	Review Hearings	Permanency Planning Hearing
			DIMENSIONS		
			Investigation		
			Consultation		
			Assessment		
			Identifying the child's interests		
			Permanency planning		
			Client counseling		
			Decision making		
			Problem solving		
			Identifying action steps		
			Follow-up		

Thus, at disposition the court officially considers what it shall do to protect and help the child and his or her family.

The court considers what orders it shall enter to deal with the unfitness of the child's home environment. In nearly every jurisdiction, the focus is on developing a case plan that sets forth the actions to be taken by the parents, the agency, and other professionals to achieve rehabilitation of the family situation.

Although state laws vary somewhat, most require a case plan that includes elements required by federal law for children in foster care supported by federal funds. If placement of the child is recommended with someone other than the child's parent, guardian, or custodian, the agency is required to document that reasonable efforts have been made to prevent or eliminate the need for the child's removal from home or to make it possible for the child to return home. The law also requires that the case plan:

1. Describe the type and appropriateness of placement.

2. Discuss how the agency responsible for the child will carry out the judicial determination regarding the child.

3. Present a plan for ensuring that the child receives proper care and that services are provided to the parents, child, and foster parents.

4. Describe how such services are to improve the conditions in the parents' home to facilitate return of the child to his or her own home or the permanent placement of the child.

5. Include a discussion of how the plan is designed to achieve a placement in the least restrictive (most family-like) setting available and in close proximity to the home of the parent(s), consistent with the best interests and special needs of the child.

6. Describe the services offered or provided and the reasonable efforts made to help the child remain with the family or to return home.

7. Is to be developed within a reasonable period but in no event later than sixty days after the agency assumes responsibility for providing services or placing the child.

The child advocate can play a significant role in ensuring that the case plan is specific and addresses the needs of the child and family. The case plan can serve to integrate the legal and social aspects of the case and provides the basis upon which the case is reviewed at subsequent hearings (see figure 10–2).

As at other stages of the process, cooperative settlement remains a priority for the child advocate. The advocate often plays a role in achieving cooperative and non-adversarial agreement on the case plan and the dispositional order.

**Figure 10-2. Dimensions of Child Advocacy:
Leading to the Case Plan**

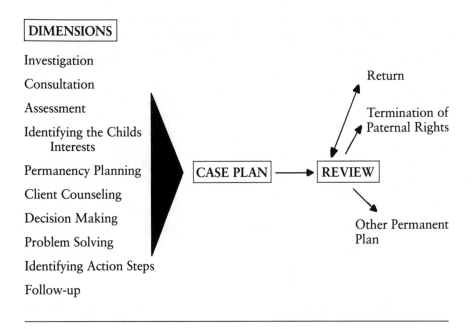

The Dimensions

Investigation and Fact Finding

- Have any significant new developments occurred since the last hearing?

In making follow-up telephone calls ten days after the trial, the advocate learned from the social worker that Ms. Hunt had been evaluated by a local psychiatrist. The results of the evaluation would be sent directly to the court. The psychiatrist up to this point had interviewed only Ms. Hunt, but she requested that the court allow her to evaluate Timmy and Ms. Hunt together, as well as speak with Timmy's aunt.

In a separate conversation with Timmy's aunt, the advocate found that she was very concerned about her family's financial situation. Apparently her husband was going to be laid off from the local automobile manufacturing plant at the end of next month.

Consultation

- What do the social worker, and other professionals involved in the case think the major problems are? What do they think should happen?
- What do the parents and other family members think the major problems are? What do they think should happen?
- What do the advocate's professionals think the major problems are? What do they think should happen?

The opinions of the parties as to what ought to happen had not changed. The social worker told the advocate that she had allowed Ms. Hunt's lawyer to choose the psychiatrist to evaluate Ms. Hunt. She now felt he was attempting to manipulate the legal process by choosing a psychiatrist who was known always to support placement of children with their biological parents.

The advocate, concerned about the financial situation of Timmy's aunt, decided to investigate possible sources of financial help for her family. The social worker informed him that the aunt was entitled to room and board payments for Timmy from the court. The court, in turn, would assess all or a portion of the costs to Ms. Hunt on an ability-to-pay basis.

Assessment

- Does the court have sufficient information and professional advice about the child, the family and the presenting problems?
- What other assessment or professional evaluation is needed?
- Who will do what, when?

The advocate was allowed to review the results of Ms. Hunt's psychiatric evaluation. The report stated that Ms. Hunt had been exposed to severe neglect as a child and possible sexual abuse by her stepfather. The psychiatrist believed that she was very attached to Timmy and was capable of supplying him with nurturance and love. She recommended that Ms. Hunt begin a supportive psychotherapy process in order to deal with her past history of abuse and neglect. In addition, she felt that Ms. Hunt would benefit most from having Timmy placed with her. Before this occurred, she wanted to evaluate Timmy and his mother together, as well as perform a family assessment within the home of Timmy's aunt.

The advocate did not support any further evaluations by this psychiatrist, especially one involving Timmy. Further, he felt it was unnecessary to do a family assessment of the aunt's family. The advocate was concerned about the psychiatrist's apparent lack of objectivity and reputation for bias in favor of natural parents. He did feel that it would be beneficial to have Ms. Hunt and Timmy evaluated by an independent court-appointed psychologist or psychiatrist rather than one selected by her own lawyer.

Identifying the Child's Interests

- Is the child protected from physical and emotional harm?
- Is the child provided adequate food, clothing, shelter, guidance, and supervision?
- Have all reasonable efforts been made to protect the child in the home?
- If the child is placed, does the placement disrupt the child's life as little as possible?
- Is the placement in the least restrictive (most family-like) setting?
- Are regular and frequent visits with the parent(s) arranged?
- Is the case proceeding in a timely manner?
- Are necessary services being promptly provided to the child and family?

Timmy's interests remained unchanged from the day of the trial. His aunt was meeting his daily needs, although she worried about not being able to afford to care for him once her husband was laid off. She also was concerned about his continued aggressiveness toward her youngest son. The advocate thought that Timmy might need therapy to help him deal with his feelings and past abuse. He decided to ask the court to explore this possibility, especially since the aunt could no longer afford to pay for the therapy.

Timmy's aunt supported the continuing contact between Timmy and his mother. She told the advocate that the visits were going well; however, Ms. Hunt was beginning to speak more definitively about wanting Timmy back soon. Timmy continued to say that he wanted to live in his aunt's home.

Permanency Planning

- Are there people familiar to the child, such as relatives and friends or neighbors, who could care for him or her?
- What steps can be taken to disrupt the normal pattern of the child's life as little as possible?
- How long is the placement likely to continue? Is the current placement available for as long as the child might need to be in placement?
- Has frequent visitation been arranged, or is there compelling reason not to allow visits between parent(s) and child?

Timmy's aunt remained willing to keep Timmy for as long as necessary, but she was beginning to worry about the financial stress and possible injury to her youngest child. Visits between Timmy and Ms. Hunt were continuing, with the aunt specifically saying she would encourage them.

Timmy's need for stability was being met by remaining in his aunt's home, but the placement could not be taken for granted. The stability was threatened from several quarters: his aggressive acting out toward his cousin, the financial difficulties of his aunt and uncle, and the ongoing, inevitable, and probably desirable stress of Ms. Hunt's visits. If Timmy's life were not to be disrupted the court would have to help arrange psychological counseling for him. In addition, the advocate was continuing to investigate financial support for the family of Timmy's aunt.

Client Counseling

- Does the child have questions about the court process?
- How does the child feel about options presented by all parties to this point?
- What does the child want to see happen as a result of these proceedings?
- Where does the child want to live now?
- What other preferences does the child have about placement, visitation, school and so forth?
- What does the child want communicated to the court, social worker, or parent(s)?

The social worker and the advocate explained to Timmy that the judge would decide how long he would stay with his aunt. Ms. Hunt's lawyer was pushing to have Timmy return to his mother as soon as possible.

Timmy wanted to continue to stay with his aunt and wanted the advocate to tell the judge so.

Decision Making and Coming to a Tentative Position

- What should the advocate be prepared to recommend to the court?
- What are the goals of the advocate at this time?

The child advocate adhered to the goal of having Timmy stay with is aunt for the short-term future. A guardianship was a means of achieving that goal but a temporary wardship under the supervision of the juvenile court would have the advantage of ongoing supervision and support by the court, the social worker, and the child advocate.

The advocate was aware that Ms. Hunt probably would contest the continued placement with the aunt. Her lawyer would use the results of her psychiatric evaluation to show that she was a fit mother and should have custody of Timmy in the near future. The advocate continued to have doubts about her ability to be an effective parent but was encouraged by her decision to enter psychotherapy. Ms. Hunt was aware that Timmy's aunt faced an uncertain financial future and would probably bring this up in court.

After consultation with the supervising attorney, the advocate decided that temporary juvenile court wardship was in Timmy's best interests. In addition, he felt that an independent psychological examination of Ms. Hunt was necessary, and he decided to ask the court to arrange for psychological counseling for Timmy.

Finally, the advocate resolved to ask the court to make room and board payments to the aunt for Timmy.

Problem Solving and Mediation

- What are the common interests among the parties?
- Can the advocate promote a cooperative resolution of any problems?
- What other institutions besides child welfare and the courts can assist in addressing any problems?

The advocate felt that all parties desired to see Timmy returned ultimately to his mother; however, the timetable differed among the participants. The advocate tried to persuade Ms. Hunt and her attorney to agree to placing Timmy with his aunt for three months. This would allow Ms. Hunt to complete her independent psychological evaluation, as well as progress in her therapy. Timmy's aunt thought that she could support Timmy's living with her family for at least the next month or two while her husband was laid off, especially if the court could provide some financial assistance.

Identifying Action Steps

- What needs to be done to protect the child?
- What action does the advocate want the court to take?
- What action should the social worker take?
- What action should others take?
- Who is to do what, when? What services does the family need? How will these services be provided? by whom? when?

On the day of the dispositional hearing, all parties entered the courtroom before the judge. Ms. Hunt's lawyer presented her psychiatric evaluation and asked that Timmy be turned over immediately to his mother's custody. The child welfare agency attorney objected to the validity of the evaluation on the grounds that it was not carried out by an unbiased professional. The judge asked the social worker why his order for an independent assessment was not carried out. The social worker informed the judge that she did not know the psychiatrist and had assumed she was acceptable to all parties. The judge asked the social worker to arrange another assessment with one of the psychologists normally used by the court.

The child advocate told the court that Timmy desired to be placed with his aunt. He believed it best that Timmy continue as a juvenile court ward placed with his aunt. He asked for room and board payments to the aunt for Timmy's care and suggested that the court review this decision in three months. Ms. Hunt's attorney objected to this plan and questioned the financial stability of Timmy's aunt.

The judge asked the aunt about her financial situation, and she explained about her husband's layoff. The advocate also informed the court of Timmy's need for psychological counseling.

The court ruled that Timmy's aunt would have temporary custody, to be reviewed in three months. The judge directed the social worker to help arrange for Timmy to be seen in counseling through a public mental health clinic. The judge supported Ms. Hunt's decision to enter therapy and asked her to have her therapist send him a report of her progress in time for the review hearing. Room and board payments were to be made by the court to the aunt for Timmy's care. Ms. Hunt was ordered to reimburse the court thirty dollars per week—a portion of the total cost.

Follow-up

- Identify steps to be taken by the advocate and others before the next court appearance.
- Contact the principals either in person or by telephone to get the steps accomplished.
- Keep a tickler system of reminders of important follow-up steps.

The child advocate followed up on the implementation of the dispositional order by calling Timmy's aunt on a monthly basis. He checked with the aunt to assess her financial situation, Timmy's counseling, and the progress of Timmy's visits with his mother. In addition, he contacted the social worker monthly to check on the status of Mrs. Hunt's psychological evaluation and therapy.

11
Review Hearings

The Legal Context

After the court enters dispositional orders, the case is brought back before the court on a regular basis for review. The review hearings generally focus on the case plan and whether it has been properly implemented and whether it has had or is having the desired effect. In determining whether the case plan developed at the dispositional hearing has been followed, the court wants to know not only what the parents have done for themselves to reestablish a home for their child but also what the social agency has done to facilitate that progress. The parents are given a fair opportunity to correct the problems that brought the child before the court.

A central question at the review hearing is what additional actions, if any, need to be taken by the parent, guardian, or agency to correct the conditions that caused the child to be placed in foster care or to remain in foster care. The review hearing should end with an amended case plan that specifies what the parents are to do and when and what other agencies and professionals will do and when. (See figure 11–1.)

The Dimensions

Investigation and Fact Finding

The advocate will have monitored the case progress up to the review hearing, but two weeks or so before the hearing, he or she should make a round of telephone calls to the social worker, foster parents, natural parents, attorneys, and others involved in the case. The lay advocate working with a lawyer should follow a lawyer's code of professional ethics and not contact the parents directly without permission of the parents' lawyer. The advocate used the case plan from the dispositional hearing as a checklist to determine what progress has been made.

**Figure 11–1. Dimensions of Child Advocacy
in the Child Protection Legal Process: Review Hearings**

Preliminary Hearing	Pretrial Conference	Trial	Dispositional Hearing	**REVIEW HEARINGS**	Permanency Planning Hearing
				DIMENSIONS	
				Investigation	
				Consultation	
				Assessment	
				Identifying the child's interests	
				Permanency planning	
				Client counseling	
				Decision making	
				Problem solving	
				Identifying action steps	
				Follow-up	

- Using the case plan as a checklist, the advocate should inquire as to significant new developments since the dispositional hearing.
- What progress has been made toward alleviating the conditions that caused the child to be placed in foster care or that cause the child to remain in foster care?
- If the child is placed with the parents, what progress has been made toward alleviating the conditions that cause him or her to remain under court supervision?

The advocate contacted the social worker and found that Ms. Hunt's psychiatrist had forwarded a favorable report of her progress in therapy. In addition, the independent psychological evaluation of Ms. Hunt indicated that she was capable of providing nurturance and love to her child but seemed to have difficulty expressing her anger appropriately. The psychologist recommended that Ms. Hunt continue in psychotherapy to resolve this problem. Also, the report stated that if this issue was addressed and worked on, then Timmy would be safe in his mother's custody, although not beforehand.

Timmy's aunt told the advocate that Timmy's counseling had helped to eliminate most of his aggressive behavior toward her youngest son. Her financial situation had not improved. Her husband's unemployment assistance was expected to end within the next three to four months, and there did not appear to be any chance of his being recalled for work in the near future. They were receiving monthly checks from the court for Timmy's care, however. Timmy's aunt continued to support Timmy's visits with his mother and stated that Timmy was becoming less afraid of being alone with her.

Consultation

- What do the social worker, and other professionals involved in the case think of the progress made? What do they think should happen?
- What do the advocate's professionals think of the progress made on the case? What do they think should happen?

The social worker was encouraged by Ms. Hunt's progress in therapy and her positive evaluation. The advocate's supervising attorney suggested that he investigate whether Timmy's aunt could care for him for another three months. In addition, the advocate decided to contact Ms. Hunt and her lawyer for permission to speak with Ms. Hunt's psychiatrist about her therapy process.

Assessment

- Does the court have sufficient information and professional advice about the child, the family, and the presenting problems?
- In the light of the experience since the last hearing, what other assessment or professional evaluation is needed?
- Who will do what, when?

The advocate decided that no further assessments were needed. He was, however, interested in speaking with the therapists of Ms. Hunt and Timmy to determine how prepared each was for the possible placement of Timmy with his mother.

Identifying the Child's Interests

- Is the child protected from physical and emotional harm?
- Is the child provided adequate food, clothing, shelter, guidance, and supervision?
- Have all reasonable efforts been made to protect the child in his own home?
- If the child is placed, does the placement disrupt the child's life as little as possible
- Is the placement in the least restrictive (most family-like) setting?

- Are regular and frequent visits with the parent(s) arranged?
- Is the case proceeding in a timely manner?
- Are necessary services being promptly provided to the child and family?

The advocate believed that Timmy's interests were served best by remaining with his aunt for the short term. He doubted, however, given the financial and personal pressures of her husband's long-term unemployment, whether the aunt would support continued placement with her after the three-month arrangement.

Ms. Hunt remained romantically involved with a man who had a successful long-distance trucking business and wanted to support Timmy and his mother.

Permanency Planning

- Is the child's home safe, or can it be made safe pending further proceedings?
- What reasonable efforts can be made to prevent or eliminate the need for out-of-home placement?
- Is the normal pattern of the child's life disrupted as little as possible?
- How long is the placement likely to continue? Is the current placement available for as long as the child might need to be in placement?
- Has frequent visitation been arranged, or is there compelling reason not to allow visits between parent and child?
- Is adequate progress being made toward permanency for the child?

The advocate received permission to contact Ms. Hunt's psychiatrist who told the advocate that Ms. Hunt had made significant progress in dealing with her own history of abuse and was beginning to express her anger appropriately. The psychiatrist felt Ms. Hunt could adequately care for Timmy at this time, especially with the support of her boyfriend.

Timmy's counselor informed the advocate that Timmy was beginning to accept his mother as a maternal figure, although he still viewed his aunt as the main adult figure in his life. The counselor did not support any type of move for Timmy in the near future since he was forming a few friendships and the therapy was going well.

The visits between Timmy and his mother had become very pleasant and were still supported by the aunt. The aunt, however, was not sure that she would be able to care for Timmy after her husband's unemployment benefits ran out. She did not say she definitely could not care for the boy, but she was increasingly concerned.

Client Counseling

- Does the child have questions about the court process?
- What does the child want to see happen as a result of these proceedings?
- Where does the child want to live now?
- How does the child feel about the options presented by all parties to this point.
- What other preferences does the child have about placement, visitation, school, and so forth?
- What does the child want communicated to the court, social worker, or parent(s)?

The advocate visited with Timmy and spoke with him about the upcoming review hearing. By now, Timmy was very familiar with the court process and did not have any related questions. He continued to want to live with his aunt although now said he would entertain the possibility of someday living with his mother. Timmy was happy in his school and spoke to the advocate about his new friends.

Although the advocate had other options and questions in his mind about future directions the case could take, none seemed likely enough to warrant discussing them with Timmy. At this point significant progress was being made toward the goals of the case plan established at the dispositional hearing. Discussing options such as termination of parental rights or foster care, as unlikely as they seemed at this point, would only upset Timmy unnecessarily.

Decision Making and Coming to a Tentative Position

- What should the advocate be prepared to recommend to the court?
- What additional services does the advocate think are necessary to rectify the conditions that caused the child to be placed in foster care or to remain in foster care?
- What additional actions does the advocate think need to be taken by the parent or guardian, to correct the conditions that caused the child to be placed in foster care or to remain in foster care?
- Should the advocate recommend that the child be returned home?
- Should the advocate recommend steps be taken toward termination of parental rights or some other permanent plan away from the natural parents?
- What are the goals of the advocate at this time?

The advocate spoke with his supervising attorney about the aunt's precarious financial situation and the possibility of returning Timmy to his mother's custody rather than finding another placement for him in the local community. The advocate tentatively decided to recommend that Timmy be placed with his mother at the end of the school year in three months if she continued to progress in therapy, was able to establish a permanent residence in Michigan, and was successful in increased visitation privileges over this time period. If this could not be agreed upon by Ms. Hunt and her lawyer, the advocate was prepared to recommend placement with a foster family if the aunt could not continue caring for Timmy and if Timmy was agreeable.

Problem Solving and Mediation

- What are the common interests among the parties?
- Can the advocate promote a cooperative resolution of any of these problems?

Through a series of telephone calls, the advocate discussed the plan of returning Timmy to his mother with the social worker, Timmy's aunt, and Ms. Hunt. They all agreed it was a good idea if the details could be worked out.

Timmy's aunt told the advocate that her husband was still unemployed, with no sign of a change in the near future. Ms. Hunt agreed to all of the stipulations for her regaining custody except to her remaining in Michigan. However, she did state that she would not move until both she and Timmy had finished therapy.

Identifying Action Steps

- What needs to be done to protect the child?
- What action does the advocate want the court to take?
- What action should the social worker take?
- What action should others take?
- Who is to do what, when? What services does the family need? How will these services be provided? by whom? when?

When the parties entered the courtroom for the review hearing before the judge, the advocate recommended that Timmy be placed with his mother in three months—at the end of the current school year. The advocate stated to the court that he believed this was the best situation for Timmy at the present time. In addition, Timmy's mother had agreed to remain in Michigan while he finished his counseling and she completed her therapy.

In order to ease Timmy's transition to his mother's custody, the social worker recommended, with the advocate's concurrence, a gradual process of extended visitation with his mother and, once placed with his mother, visitation with the aunt's family.

Ms. Hunt's lawyer asked for immediate placement with his client in the light of the favorable reports the judge had received from her evaluation and psychiatrist. In addition, he told the court that Ms. Hunt and her boyfriend were renting an apartment that was quite adequate for Timmy.

The court ruled that Timmy would be returned to his mother in three months if she agreed to remain in Michigan for an additional period of supervised home placement. The judge complemented Ms. Hunt on her effort in working to regain custody. He set a review hearing for six months hence. He would follow the case through the reports from the Department of Social Services, which would indicate Ms. Hunt's progress in therapy, the state of her permanent residence, whether her relationship with Timmy was satisfactory, and whether Timmy's well-being was being looked after. The judge ordered a gradually increasing visitation schedule for Ms. Hunt that would lead to her having Timmy stay at her residence for five days at a time, with full physical custody in three months, at the end of the school year. He also ordered that Timmy's aunt be allowed to visit him at least weekly once Ms. Hunt regained custody. The court date, six months hence was to finalize Timmy's return to his mother's custody and consider dismissing court jurisdiction. Any party could request an earlier hearing date.

Follow-up

- Identify steps to be taken by the advocate and others before the next court appearance.
- Contact principals either in person or by telephone to get the steps accomplished.
- Keep a tickler system of reminders of important follow-up steps.

The advocate stayed in monthly contact with Timmy's aunt, Ms. Hunt and the social services worker supervising the case to ensure that Timmy's best interests were being looked after. Timmy's aunt was very supportive of the court's decision, and Timmy gradually adjusted to spending more time with his mother. The advocate spoke with Timmy regularly to determine his feelings about the recent developments. Timmy finally wanted to return to his mother's care and looked forward to moving back with her full time. At the end of the three-month period, the transition from the aunt's home to Ms. Hunt's new residence was smooth.

Timmy as returned to his mother's custody. She married the man with whom she had been living for the past two years. At the review hearing, Timmy was doing well, and the case was dismissed.

The family moved out-of-state shortly afterward to follow business opportunities of the stepfather. The aunt's husband eventually was called back to work. Timmy and his mother remain on good terms with the aunt.

12
Permanency Planning Hearing

The Legal Context

Federal Law

In 1980, after years of discussion and debate about the nation's child welfare and foster care system, the U.S. Congress enacted Public Law (PL) 96-272, the Adoption Assistance and Child Welfare Act of 1980 (42 USC §675). Congress wanted to encourage the states to adopt law reforms that would reduce the number of children placed in foster care by protecting children at home with natural parents if at all possible. If a child were removed from the biological family, the law was intended to see that rehabilitative services were focused on the family in a fairly short period of time (less than eighteen months) so that if the child could be returned to the biological family, it would be done as soon as possible. Congress believed that the foster care system was too easy for a child to enter but quite difficult to exit so that large numbers of children were growing up in temporary foster care, sometimes in a succession of temporary foster placements, without permanent homes. Congress made state eligibility for federal foster care funds conditional on the state's enacting certain procedures. Most states, by statute, court rule, or administrative procedure, have adopted the federal procedures.

Among the federal requirements of PL 96-272 is that the state hold a permanency planning hearing or permanency review after a youngster has been in foster care for eighteen months. Some states hold the permanency review after twelve months in care. The hearing is intended to be a decision point at which the agency or the court determines whether efforts to rehabilitate the family are likely to be successful. If not, an alternative permanent plan is to be sought—most commonly termination of parental rights so that the child may be adopted.

A decision point—a "fish or cut bait" hearing—was considered necessary because so many children were deprived of the stability and security of a permanent family because of temporizing and indecision. These children were neither returned to their biological family nor placed permanently, through guardianship or adoption, with another family. Instead they drifted in foster care, belonging nowhere and often not achieving a sense of place and roots.

Although each state's procedures vary somewhat, there are similarities. Essentially the court (or the agency) must determine whether the youngster can be returned to the care of the biological parents now or in the near future. If the decision is to sever the relationship, legal procedures to achieve permanency for the child apart from the family of origin must be initiated. Most commonly those procedures are for termination of parental rights, but occasionally long-term placement with relatives or guardianship or even long-term foster care achieves the desired legal and psychological permanence for the child.

The permanency hearing can be very important for the child because it can resolve an uncertain state of limbo in foster care. The decision to seek termination of parental rights or to return a child to a home that is far from ideal, and perhaps not even minimally adequate, is difficult for all concerned. It is very tempting to avoid the hard decisions presented. Judges, social workers, lawyers, and others often find it easier to make no decision rather than face the difficult choices presented. The child, however, can suffer as much from no decision as from a wrong decision. The advocate can play an important role in pressing for a permanency resolution after a period in foster care.

State Law

The Michigan permanency planning statute is illustrative of state procedures enacted to conform to the federal requirements. (Other states have similar requirements.) In Michigan, if a child remains in foster care for 364 days after a dispositional hearing, the court must hold a permanency planning hearing to review the status of the child and the progress made toward the child's return home or to show why the child should not be placed in the permanent custody of the court:

> (4) If parental rights to the child have not been terminated and the court determines at a permanency planning hearing that the return of the child to his or her parent would not cause a substantial risk of harm to the child's life, physical health, or mental well-being, the court shall order the child returned to his or her parent. In determining whether the return of the child would cause a substantial risk of harm to the child, the court shall view the failure of the parent to substantially comply with the terms and conditions of the case service plan prepared under section 18f of this chapter as evidence that return of the child to his or her parent would cause a substantial risk of harm to the child's life, physical health, or mental well-being.

(5) If the court determines at a permanency planning hearing that the child should not return to his or her parent, the agency shall initiate proceedings to terminate parental rights to the child not later than 42 days after the permanency planning hearing, unless the agency demonstrates to the court that initiating the termination of parental rights to the child is clearly not in the child's best interests.[1]

The permanency plannig hearing is not the same as the hearing to terminate parental rights or order guardianship or another long-term plan for the child; these actions occur subsequent to the permanency hearing. The law maintains its clear preference for placement of the child with the family of origin; only if the child remains at risk in the parents' home does the permanency hearing set the alternative course. The hearing formally marks the point at which the agency shifts from a primary emphasis on rehabilitation and reunification of the family to a primary focus on achieving an alternative permanent plan for the child.

After fully considering a petition to terminate parental rights or for another permanent plan for the child, the court may find that the case has not been made, and another round of rehabilitation or search for alternatives may be necessary. But the hope is that the momentum behind the search for permanence for the child will remain.

The advocate's role is outlined in the following case example applying the ten dimensions of advocacy to the permanency planning hearing. (See figure 12–1.)

Figure 12–1. Dimensions of Child Advocacy in the Child Protection Legal Process: Permanency Hearing

Preliminary Hearing	Pretrial Conference	Trial	Dispositional Hearing	Review Hearings	**PERMANENCY PLANNING HEARING**
					DIMENSIONS
					Investigation
					Consultation
					Assessment
					Identifying the child's interests
					Permanency planning
					Client counseling
					Decision making
					Problem solving
					Identifying action steps
					Follow-up

The Case of Jane and Monica Grey

Monica was born eighteen months ago to Jane Grey, a twenty-two year od woman hospitalized five times since age seventeen for schizophrenia.[2] Monica lived with her mother for one month until Jane came to a hospital emergency room looking for assistance. She appeared to be actively psychotic at the time and twice left the child unattended in the hospital waiting room for at least thirty minutes each time. She made threatening statements to the child, saying, "Looks like her dad and I want to hit her" and "I think I'll burn her." She was admitted to the psychiatric hospital that same day, where she stayed for two weeks. Child protective services found that Jane's father was her only family member, and he was unable to take care of the baby at that time. He also had a history of mental illness and took medication to control schizophrenia. The juvenile court ordered the baby placed temporarily in a foster home.

Juvenile court assumed formal jurisdiction of Monica Grey one month after this incident. Two men were named as possible fathers of Monica, but both denied any interest in her. Jane Grey, with the advice of counsel, entered a plea of no contest and vowed to work with the agency social worker, mental health counselors, and the court to stabilize her life and resume custody of her daughter. Monica remained in the same foster home.

The case plan developed by the agency and Jane provided that Jane was to refrain from drug or alcohol use, to continue in counseling with mental health services, to take medication as prescribed by her psychiatrist, to visit Monica on a regular basis, to conduct herself appropriately during those visits, and to participate in parenting classes. The permanency goal at this time was for Monica to be reunited with Jane within twelve months.

Jane Grey complied well with the elements of the case plan. She was a pleasant and likable person and attended all but a few of the scheduled visits with Monica, participated in her counseling program, and willingly pursued parenting classes. Despite her compliance with the case plan, however, her personal instability continued. Five months after the case plan was approved at the dispositional hearing, Jane was readmitted to a psychiatric hospital with anxiety and racing thoughts. She was released fourteen days later. Two months later, she was admitted for attempted suicide when she took an overdose of drugs.

Two parenting classes rejected Jane, saying that her problems were psychiatric and not amenable to change through their methods. A third program accepted her, and she attended faithfully. She understood intellectually all that was expected of her but still had great emotional difficulty dealing with Monica during longer visits at the social agency. After interacting with Monica for a short period of time, she preferred to talk with other adults in the room—her father, the casework aide, and the caseworker. She was often inattentive to Monica even during the supervised visits despite the fact that it was repeatedly explained to her that she was expected to provide the primary care. For instance, Jane would not change

Monica's diaper until the aide or caseworker brought it to Jane's attention. Monica occassionally needed assistance with toys or with her bottle, and Jane did not seem to notice without assistance. She said that she was not sure she even wanted Monica back in her care. "It's scary, to think of having custody of Monica," she said at one point.

This was the situation at the third quarterly review hearing before the judge, nine months after the dispositional hearing. At that hearing, the social worker recommended that an evaluation be arranged by a university-based multi-disciplinary team that specialized in difficult foster care cases. The child advocate supported this idea, and the court ordered that it be done. In making the referral the worker asked the team to address two questions:

1. Is Jane Grey capable of parenting Monica now or in the next year?
2. What intervention plan should be offered to make reunification possible? Are there specific therapy or casework recommendations?

The evaluation of the multidisciplinary team and the history to this point provided the background for the child advocate for the permanency planning hearing. Monica has been in foster care for seventeen of her eighteen months of life. The child advocate's permanency review began two weeks before the scheduled court hearing. He had reviewed the reports from the university multidisciplinary team and arranged to meet with the social worker.

The Dimensions

Investigation and Fact Finding

- Using the case plan as a checklist, the advocate should inquire as to significant new developments since the last hearing.
- What progress has been made toward alleviating the conditions that caused the child to be placed in foster care or that cause the child to remain in foster care?
- If the child is placed with his or her parents, what progress has been made toward alleviating the conditions that cause him or her to remain under the supervision of the court?

The difficulty with this case was that Jane Grey, an intelligent, likable young woman, was complying with the elements of the case plan nearly to the letter—but without benefiting from them. The multidisciplinary team observations of Jane and Monica together were consistent with the experience so far. Jane seemed somewhat distant from Monica and easily stressed, to the point of being overwhelmed by her.

Jane had the assistance of a job training program and after training and counseling was placed in three different positions with help from a job coach. But she was unable to deal with the repeated demands on her, even minimal ones, and quit each job within three days.

It appears that the original conditions that caused Monica to come under the supervision of the court, Jane Grey's mental illness, continued with little progress.

Consultation

- What do the parents, social worker, and other professionals involved in the case think of the progress made on the case? What do they think should happen?
- What do the advocate's supervising professionals think of the progress made on the case? What do they think should happen?
- What additional services are necessary to rectify the conditions that caused the child to be placed in foster care or to remain in foster care?

The multidisciplinary team assessment determined that Jane Grey was unable to be an effective parent to Monica at the present time and that she would likely be unable to do so at any time in the future. Despite her pleasant attitude and intelligence, the team felt that Jane's psychiatric condition was chronic and that other psychotic episodes were probable should she be stressed. Her inability to handle the modest stresses of working in a bakery, restaurant, and hospital accounts office were seen as an index for her ability to take care of her child, which would be equally, if not more, stressful. Her ambivalence toward Monica and her inability to form and maintain close relationships also were noted. Her only family member, her father, was not necessarily a positive force in her life and could not provide the ongoing support necessary to allow Jane to assume custody of Monica. The team, reluctantly but firmly, recommended that counselors work with Jane to help her release Monica for adoption voluntarily. Should that fail, they recommended involuntary termination of parental rights.

On the other hand, Jane's mental health therapists said she was stabilizing and making good progress. Although she could not assume care of Monica in the next few months, they felt that she had a good chance of being able to care for Monica in the future, with some ongoing help.

The foster care worker was quite torn as to what course to take. She like Jane, who she felt was trying her best. On the other hand, Monica could not wait forever for her mother to be stable enough to care for her. The worker could think of no additional services to try. Without a supportive family who could live with

Jane and Monica, there was no other way the worker could think living with Jane could be safe for Monica. Yet she hesitated coming to a decision. In part she was hoping something would happen to show a way to reunite the mother and daughter.

The advocate conferred with his supervising attorney and learned that under the laws of this state, parental rights could be terminated based on a parent's failure to provide proper care and custody and inability to do so within a reasonable time considering the age of the child. A judge could find that Monica's situation warranted termination of parental rights, but it was by no means a clear-cut case, especially with a parent as sympathetic and cooperative as Jane Grey.

Assessment

- Does the court have sufficient information and professional advice about the child, the family, and the presenting problems?
- In the light of the experience since the last hearing, what other assessment or professional evaluation is needed?

Except for Jane's lawyer, no one the advocate consulted thought that additional evaluation was necessary. Jane's lawyer thought the university team might be biased in favor of termination and said he would ask the court to order an evaluation by a psychologist of his own choosing.

Identifying the Child's Interests

- Is the child protected from physical and emotional harm?
- Is the child provided adequate food, clothing, shelter, guidance, and supervision?
- Are regular and frequent visits arranged?
- Are necessary services being promptly provided to the child and family?

Monica had been placed directly in the Taylor foster home at one month of age and has remained there ever since. The Taylors have taken Monica to visit with Jane, and occasionally Jane has visited Monica in the Taylor home. Monica has lived with the Taylors longer than with Jane. At this point no additional services have been suggested for Jane and Monica.

Permanency Planning

- Is the child's home safe or can it be made safe pending further proceedings?

- Is the normal pattern of the child's life disrupted as little as possible?
- How long is the placement likely to continue? Is the current placement available for as long as the child might need it?
- Has frequent visitation been arranged, or is there compelling reason not to allow visits between parent and child?
- Is adequate progress being made toward permanency for the child?

Despite the best efforts of the agency, the Grey home is still not safe for Monica. Jane's mental condition seemed too precarious to allow overnight visits, although there have been twice-weekly visits from the beginning of the case. The Taylors are willing to keep Monica for as long as necessary, and, when asked by the caseworker, they said they would be interested in adopting her should she become available.

Indecision still reigns with the caseworker and Jane Grey as to a long-range plan for Monica.

Client Counseling

- Does the child have questions about the court process?
- What does the child want to see happen as a result of these proceedings?
- Where does the child want to live now?
- How does the child feel about the options presented by all parties to this point?
- What other preferences does the child have about placement, visitation, school, and so forth?
- What does the child want communicated to the court, social worker, or parent?

Since Monica is only eighteen months old, there is little by way of client counseling required. The advocate has visited her in the foster parents' home, and she seems healthily attached to them. She is somewhat wary and ill at ease with her mother, but that is not surprising in that Jane has had custody for such a short period.

Decision Making and Coming to a Tentative Position

- What additional services does the advocate think are necessary to rectify the conditions that caused the child to be placed in or remain in foster care?

- What additional actions does the advocate think need to be taken by the parent or guardian to correct the conditions that caused the child to be placed in or remain in foster care?
- Should the advocate recommend return of the child home?
- Should the advocate recommend steps be taken toward termination of parental rights or some other permanent plan away from the natural parents?
- What are the goals of the advocate at this time?
- What should the advocate be prepared to recommend to the court?

The caseworker has strongly identified with Jane Grey and is reluctant to turn away from trying to reunite her and Monica. The advocate therefore believes that if he does not press for filing a termination of parental rights petition, no one else will. His supervising attorney has often warned him that the "best interests of the child" are not a ground for termination in this state. As a psychological matter, however, the best interests of Monica are probably served by being adopted by the Taylors. Monica might be better served if she could know who her biological mother is as she is growing up with some opportunity for occasional visits.

The advocate can think of no additional services for Monica and her mother except to continue the support and therapy through mental health and hope that those services are more successful in the next few months than they have been. Unlike other cases, the agency services in this matter have been excellent. Jane's precarious mental condition, as evidenced by her job performance, visits with Monica, suicide attempts, and rehospitalizations, appears to preclude a recommendation of returning Monica to her mother at this time.

The advocate decides to take the tentative position of recommending that a petition to terminate parental rights be filed. In the meantime he will try to achieve a settlement, perhaps through a voluntary release of rights and an open adoption arrangement.

Problem Solving and Mediation

- What are the common interests among the parties?
- Can the advocate promote a cooperative resolution of any of these problems?

Jane Grey has said that if she cannot have custody of Monica, she would like the Taylors to adopt her child. In fact, her feelings of inadequacy when comparing herself to the Taylors led the caseworker to stop Jane's visits at the foster home;

instead she or case aides transported Monica to other locations for visits.

Jane's appreciation of the Taylors and her ambivalence toward regaining custody prompted the advocate to ask her attorney and the caseworker to pursue a settlement in which Jane would voluntarily release Monica for adoption. Under this state's law, foster parents have the first opportunity to adopt. The Taylors were agreeable to maintaining contact with Jane should they adopt, thinking the relationship would be good for Monica. An open adoption in which parents retained visiting rights even after the adoption was not provided for in the law of this state, but an informal agreement for ongoing contact would be possible.

When Jane's attorney first presented this idea to her, she was initially quite interested. After thinking it over, and talking with her father and counselors, however, she could not bring herself to agree to it.

Jane remained interested, though ambivalent, about voluntary release of the child and at the permanency hearing asked for a recess to reconsider the option. After conferences with her attorney and therapist, she again declined the option.

Settlement was close but not realized. Nonetheless, those discussions contributed to an atmosphere in later proceedings that was child centered, respectful of Jane Grey, and not harshly adversarial in tone.

Identifying Action Steps

- What needs to be done to protect the child?
- What action does the advocate want the court to take?
- What action should the social worker take?
- What action should others take?
- Who is to do what, when? What services does the family need? How will these services be provided? by whom? when?

At the hearing, the advocate recommended that Monica not be returned to her mother and that a petition to terminate parental rights be filed by the agency.

The caseworker, in part because of discussions with the advocate, also recommended that Monica remain in foster care and said the agency would file a petition to terminate parental rights.

After hearing testimony, the court determined that the child could not be returned to her mother's custody. The caseworker and her lawyer were obliged under law to prepare a case and file a petition in a short time.

Visits between Jane and Monica were continued pending the termination hearing.

Follow-up

- Identify the steps to be taken by the advocate and others before the next court appearance.

- Contact principals either in person or by telephone to get the steps accomplished.
- Keep a ticker system of reminders of important follow-up steps.

The advocate's supervising attorney would have primary responsibility for the termination of parental rights hearing, but the advocate listed steps he needed to take:

1. Brief the supervising lawyer on Monica's case and the reasons for termination of parental rights. Encourage the lawyer to collaborate with the agency attorney.
2. Call the caseworker in two weeks to check on progress in drafting the petition.

Monica's case went to termination hearing. Expert testimony from the multidisciplinary team on the chronic and delicate nature of Jane Grey's mental condition was central. Twice during the two-day hearing, Jane Grey came close to voluntarily releasing her rights.

At the end, the court took the matter under advisement and three weeks later issued an opinion and order for termination. Jane Grey did not appeal. She seemed relieved that the questions were resolved. The Taylors will adopt Monica; they plan to encourage continued contact between Monica and Jane Grey.

Notes

1. Michigan Compiled Laws Annotated (MCLA) 712A.19.
2. The case example is based on several actual cases with similar fact patterns. The names and other identifying information have been changed to protect confidentiality.

III
Key Questions about Specific Problems

In this part, we address issues and present descriptions, background information, case scenarios of various types of abuse and neglect, and a list of key questions for advocates to use in gathering information, making decisions, and forming recommendations in particular cases. This part is designed to provide advocates with a working knowledge of some of the forms that abuse or neglect might take and define some of the pertinent terminology. Descriptions relating to the detection and/or diagnosis of abuse and neglect are presented; however, we do not expect the advocate to adopt a diagnostic role, and, indeed, we caution against this. We view the role of the advocate as one of a consumer of information and consider the advocate's ability to draw on the expertise of others to be a most valuable skill.

Chapter 16 is designed to prepare advocates to fulfill the mediation and conciliation role more effectively. Finally we present a discussion of some common barriers to effective advocacy.

13

Physical Abuse

The battered-child syndrome first gained wide public attention in the early 1960s. Kempe proposed this term in order to highlight the seriousness of the problem.[1] A pediatrician, he had observed an alarming increase in the number of children who suffered from nonaccidental injuries.[2] The following description explains the urgency Kempe felt in bringing this problem to public attention:

> Jody was four years old when her parents brought her to Colorado General Hospital. She had suffered from severe child abuse all of her life and demonstrated one of the most severe cases of malnutrition that we have seen. She weighed only seventeen pounds and was covered with bruises and abrasions. Radiological studies revealed fractures of the skull, arm, and two fractures of her hands. She also presented a high intestinal obstruction due to a hematoma.[3]

Definition

Physical abuse is defined as "any nonaccidental physical injury inflicted on a child by a parent (or other caretaker) deliberately or in anger."[4] The abusive situation can be viewed as an interactive event, with three main components:

1. The personality characteristics of the parent.
2. The personality characteristics of the child that enhance the scapegoating.
3. Socioeconomic and environmental stressors that lower the frustration tolerance of the parents.[5]

There is "no consistent or homogeneous personality profile of an abusive parent."[6] There are, however, many characteristics that a majority of these adults

---

This chapter was written by Roger Lauer.

share. Abusive parents frequently have experienced some significant degree of neglect, with or without accompanying physical abuse, during their own childhoods.[7] These parents may misperceive and misinterpret the behavior of their children, and they may have expectations for their behavior that are inappropriate for their age, as the following example shows:

> Henry J. in speaking of his sixteen month old son, Johnny, said, "He knows what I mean and understands it when I say 'come here.' If he doesn't come immediately, I go and give him a gentle tug on the ear to remind him of what he's supposed to do." In the hospital it was found that Johnny's ear was lacerated and partially torn away from his head.[8]

Often a reversal of roles occurs, and the parent looks to the child as a source of reassurance, comfort, and loving.[9] When the child cannot satisfy the needs of the parent, an abusive situation may occur. Other parental factors that have been related to abuse are alcohol and drug abuse, mental retardation, recurring mental illness, divorce and single parenthood, and feelings of isolation and lack of social supports.

Personality characteristics of the child, such as a difficult temperament, may increase the possibility of scapegoating, but they are not sufficient or necessary causes for abuse. Parents are sometimes faced with restless, hyperactive children who are difficult to manage; children who were unwanted; or children born with disabilities, such as birth defects, mental retardation, or prematurity. Any of these factors may interfere with parent-child bonding and help to increase the possibility of future abuse.

Socioeconomic and environmental stressors may serve to increase the likelihood of abuse in some families. Unemployment and financial stress frequently are found in abusive families. Marital disharmony or isolation from community support systems also may contribute to a stressful family environment.

The following case study is illustrative of the number of factors that may lead to abuse:

> Ms. S., eighteen years old, was reported to protective services for alleged abuse of her two-year-old son. Protective services had an extensive file on the S. family because Ms. S. and her younger sister had been removed from their parents' home at age four and two, respectively. The parents later had their parental rights terminated. Ms. S. has been divorced from the child's father since before his birth and said her son was exactly like his father. She described her marriage to this man as a "mistake."
>
> The protective services worker noted extensive bruises and abrasions on the child's face. He had recently healed lacerations on his upper arms.
>
> The physician's report stated that there was evidence of a spiral fracture of the child's right arm and scars from what appeared to be a third-degree burn on the left buttocks.
>
> Ms. S. explained that the injuries were the result of her discipline efforts, which she considered necessary to curb the boy's excessive activity.

Describing Physical Abuse

An advocate attempting to diagnose physical abuse often can obtain significant information from the behavior of the parents. If, for example, each parent gives a different version of how a child was injured, or if the explanations provided are not consistent with the child's developmental capabilities, then abuse may be suspected. If the parents claim to be unaware of how their child was injured or cannot offer any explanation at all, the injury may have been caused by abuse. Parental delay in seeking medical attention for their injured child may indicate an attempt to cover up abuse. A parent who seems excessively anxious or over-controlled given the condition of the child, may be abusive. Finally, families that have a pattern of using multiple health providers (sometimes referred to as "doctor hopping" or "ER hopping") may be attempting to avoid being detected as abusive.[10]

The most common outward indications of physical abuse are skin injuries in various stages of healing. Bruises (rupture of small blood vessels and discoloration without a break in the skin) and abrasions (scrape or scratch) located in areas not commonly associated with accidents should arouse concern. Common accidental locations are the shins, knees, elbows, and forehead. Bruises, abrasions, and lacerations (cuts or jagged openings in the skin) on the buttocks, back, mouth, cheek, anus, genitals, and rectum are indicative of nonaccidental injury. The instrument used to inflict injury (perhaps a belt or a cord) may be detected by the shape of the bruise.[11] Any scar with an unusual shape or location may indicate abuse. Whenever scars are present with lacerations that are at different stages of healing, abuse should be suspected, as in this example:

> A three year old boy was brought to the emergency room by his parents for breathing difficulty. There were newly formed scabs covering his buttocks. His legs showed evidence of many old scars. The child was admitted immediately and classified in critical condition.[12]

Burns account for 10 percent of all child abuse injuries. There are three types of burns: first degree (such as a sunburn); second degree (there is blistering); and third degree (skin tissue is destroyed). Accidental burns—for instance, when a child spills a hot liquid on himself or herself—may be differentiated from nonaccidental burns by the pattern left on the child's skin.[13] In the case of accidents, children reflexively withdraw from the source of the burn to prevent further injury. This results in a bruise that is less deep or less severe. When it is clear that this did not occur, forced infliction is indicated. For example, the severity of the burn caused when a child accidentally places a hand in hot water is much less than when the hand is immersed forcibly for a period of time. The most frequent type of burn seen in abuse cases is cigarette burns of the palms and soles. Immersion or dunking burns from scalding water are the next most frequently witnessed.[14] Contact burns that result from a part of the body being pressed against a hot source also are common.[15]

Multiple fractures in various stages of healing may indicate child abuse. Any fracture associated with hematomas (swelling caused by a collection of blood in the space between the muscle and skin or between the brain and skull) may indicate abuse.[16] Accidental fractures occur rarely in children. Unless the child has been involved in a major trauma, such as a car accident, or it can be proved that the parent accidentally dropped the child, any fractures should be suspect. Hildebrandt indicates that the most common nonaccidental fractures are of the long bones (arms, legs, and ribs). Greenstick fractures (bone broken on one side while other side is bent) are seen most often in toddlers. If the parents minimize these injuries or deny awareness of the injury, abuse is possible. Spiral fractures (the bone twisted until it breaks) may result from the child's being jerked violently or having a limb twisted. Multiple fractures (two or more breaks of the same bone), comound fractures (bone protruding through skin), and dislocations (displacement or separation of a bone from a joint) are other possible manifestations of abuse, though they are not common.[17] The following case is illustrative:

> Billy, four years old, lived with his single mother in a welfare hotel in a major metropolitan area. He enjoyed imitating his mother as she scrubbed the bathroom floor. One day she found him scrubbing the living room rug. His mother blew up and began to beat his fingers with the brush, ignoring his screams which just infuriated her more. When she finally stopped, she had broken all of his fingers and pulled the fingernails off many of them.[18]

Head and brain injury are usually seen in children who have survived a traumatic experience such as a car accident. When a child presents with this type of injury without having been exposed to such a trauma, abuse may be suspected. Skull fractures (break in the bone of the skull), depressed fractures (bone fragments pressed into the skull cavity), concussions (a jarring injury to the brain that results in headaches, vomiting, and possible loss of consciousness), and hematomas (internal swelling) indicate that a severe blow to the head of the child has occurred.[19] Severe shaking of the child can cause internal bleeding.

Kempe has highlighted additional forms of physical abuse: ocular damage, such as injury to the retina; intentional poisoning; human bites; internal injury due to unexplained rupture of the stomach, bowel, or liver caused by being hit or kicked; genital trauma related to toilet training, and oral trauma from forced feeding.[20]

Questions for the Advocate

- What form of physical abuse did the child suffer? What are the specific details of the abusive situation? Who is accused of abusing the child? How many times did the abuse occur? Was the same person responsible each time? Where did the abuse take place?

- Obtain a copy of the medical exam (which should always be done in this type of case). What specific injuries did the child suffer? Are they consistent with nonaccidental injury? What explanation did the parent give for the injury? Is this explanation consistent with the child's developmental abilities?

- If the child has been treated by a specific doctor or emergency room, is this the same facility used on a consistent basis, or are there indications of frequent changes in place of treatment?

- Are there some other symptoms present in the child that may indicate physical abuse, such as fear, shame, embarrassment, lack of spontaneity, bedwetting, nightmares, violent fantasies, loss of appetite, or dramatic changes in behavior? What symptoms may have been present but are no longer?

- What was the precipitating incident? How did the response compare to the provocation? Is this child in continued danger of abuse at this time?

- What is the child's account of his or her injury? Is the child afraid of further repercussions if he or she talks with the child advocate? Does it appear that the child has been compelled by the abuser or others to deny the problem or tell a different story? What was the precipitating incident according to the child? Does the child blame himself or herself for the abuse?

- Has there been a past or simultaneous abuse of another child or spouse in this family? If so, where was this person treated if injured? What is the general level of violence in the household? What is the other parent's ability to protect the child against further abuse?

- What is the child's relationship to the abuser? Does the child show age-appropriate attachment to this parent? Is the abusive parent able to put the child's needs ahead of his or her own? How do the parents discipline the children? How do the parents express anger at the child?

- If an abusive situation does exist, does the abusive parent express remorse or guilt or admit blame for the incident? Does the family have a reasonable plan for solving the current situation? Is the family isolated from community support systems? What are the resources in the community available to help this family—such as home health aides, counseling for parents and/or child, parent education class, child care, job training, and alcohol or drug abuse treatment?

- What is the parents' relationship? Are they available to and supportive of each other? Are there other ongoing problems in the family, such as a history of abuse, drug or alcohol abuse, physical disability, or mental illness? How does the family deal with these problems?

- How is the child doing in school, both before and since the abuse incident? Does this child have friends? Is the child acting aggressively toward others in school or in the neighborhood?
- What does the child want?

Notes

1. H.C. Kempe et al., "The Battered Child Syndrome," *Journal of the American Medical Association* 181 (1962): 17.

2. R. Helfer and H. Kempe, *The Battered Child,* 2d Ed. (Chicago: University of Chicago Press, 1974).

3. Ibid., P. XV.

4. Wayne and Avery, *Child Abuse: Prevention and Treatment through Social Group Work,* (Boston: Charles River Books, 1980, P. 8.

5. Green et al., "Child Abuse: Pathological Syndrome of Family Interaction," *American Journal of Psychiatry* 131 (1974).

6. Scott, cited by S. Smith, ed., *The Maltreatment of Children (Baltimore: University Park Press, 1978).*

7. *Vesterdal, cited by J. Cook and R. Bowles, eds., Child Abuse: Commission and Omission* (Toronto: Butterworth, P. 1980).

8. B.F. Steele and C.B. Pollack, in Helfer and Kempe, *Battered Child,* P. 109.

9. Ibid.

10. O.L. Kerns, "The Pediatric Perspective," in Bross and Michaels, eds., *Foundations of Child Advocacy: Legal Representation of the Maltreated Child,* (Longmont, Calif.: Bookmakers Guild, 1987).

11. M.C. Hildebrant, in K.C. Fakler, ed., *Social Work with Abused and Neglected Children: A Manual of Interdisciplinary Practice* New York: Free Press, 1981).

12. DeCourcy and DeCourcy, *A Silent Tragedy: Child Abuse in the Community,* (New York: Alfred Publishing Company, 1973).

13. Hildebrandt, in Faller, *Social Work.*

14. Kerns, "Pediatric Perspective."

15. Hildebrandt, in Faller, *Social Work.*

16. Ibid.

17. Ibid.

18. DeCourcy and DeCourcy, *Silent Tragedy.*

19. Ibid.

20. Helfer and Kempe, *Battered Child.*

14
Sexual Abuse

Debbie, age sixteen, told her school counselor that her father had been having sexual intercourse with her for several years. He was an accountant with a part-time income tax business and had his office for the tax business at home in the basement next to her bedroom. He would enter her room at night and have sex with her. He vehemently denied the sexual abuse, but based upon Debbie's statements, the juvenile court took jurisdiction and placed Debbie in foster care. She felt she was being punished by the placement.

There was also a criminal investigation during which the police seized Debbie's night clothing and bed sheets. The day before the criminal trial, her father left a note for Debbie's mother to deliver to her. In it, he said he would commit suicide if she testified against him. Debbie at first refused to testify and then got on the stand and said that she had lied, that her father would only come in and talk to her at night. She said she didn't know how his semen got on the bed sheets. Later in treatment she spoke of her inability to tell the truth in court because she did not want to be responsible for her father's suicide. He was a psychologically very fragile man who well might have committed suicide.[1]

Prevalence of Child Sexual Abuse

The National Analysis of Official Child Neglect and Abuse Reporting (1977–1983) provides the major source of information about the incidence of sexual abuse in the United States. According to Faller, data from the National Analysis show an increase in all types of maltreatment reported—from 416,000 incidents in 1976[2] to 1.7 million in 1984 and also an increase in the percentage of sexual abuse cases from 3 percent in 1976 to 13 percent in 1984.[3] It is likely

---

This chapter was written by Karin Elliott.

that child sexual abuse is chronically underreported as compared to other abusive acts because of society's incest taboo and its discomfort with sexuality and because of the potentially severe consequences the perpetrator and family may face. Faller further points out that about half of the sexual abuse perpetrators in the 1984 sample were natural parents and 32 percent were step, foster, or adoptive parents.

Some evidence suggests that where female victims are concerned, the perpetrator is likely to be a relative; where the victim is a male, the perpetrator is more likely to be an acquaintance or a stranger. Single encounters may be most common, with sexual touching or fondling occurring most often.[4]

The Functions and Causes of Sexual Abuse

Faller cites four common functions of sexual abuse: an outlet for sexual feelings, an expression of angry feelings, an effort to express and receive affection, and an opportunity to exert power.[5] She states that the extent to which any sexually abusive act is motivated by each of these four functions will vary from case to case.

Although the functions identified provide an explanation for why perpetrators commit sexual abuse, we must still be concerned with identifying what situations or preconditions make children vulnerable to sexual abus. Faller and Finkelhor have developed conceptual models that attempt to identify and describe the dynamics, preconditions, and contributing factors that precipitate sexual abuse of children.[6] Faller begins by identifying characteristics of perpetrators that are prerequisites for sexual abuse, such as a sexual attraction to children, and a willingness to act on sexual feelings. She then discusses contributing factors that increase the likelihood that sexual abuse will occur—among them, cultural, environmental, individual, and family. (See figure 14–1.) Other conceptual models try to identify and explain the causes or factors precipitating child sexual abuse.[7]

Having a basic understanding of the indicators and underlying causes of sexual abuse and the functions it serves for the perpetrator can assist child advocates with identifying children at risk and making informed decisions about reporting and referring children suspected to be victims of sexual abuse.

Definitions of Sexual Abuse

States commonly define sexual abuse as any nonconsensual sexual contact. In most states, it is also acknowledged that for all offenses, a child less than seventeen years of age is legally incapable of consent. Although actual touching must occur, direct contact with the victim's body is not required; for example, touching the victim's sexual or other intimate parts through clothing is considered sexual contact. Faller provides a more general definition of sexual abuse, which focuses

Figure 14–1. Faller's Model: The Dynamics of Sexual Abuse

PREREQUISITES   CONTRIBUTING FACTORS   OUTCOME

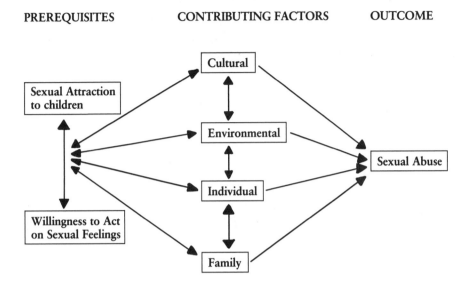

Source: K.C. Faller, *Child Sexual Abuse: An Interdisciplinary Manual for Diagnosis, Case Management and Treatment,* Copyright C. 1988, Columbia University Press, New York. Used by permission.

on how the victim experiences the sexual behavior.[8] She defines sexual abuse as "any act occurring between people who are at different developmental stages which is for the sexual gratification of the person at the more advanced developmental stage." Relatedly, child sexual maltreatment has occurred whenever a child becomes a victim of sexual assault due to the failure of the parent, or person legally responsible for the care of the child, to exercise a minimum degree of care or proper supervision.

Reporting Sexual Abuse

Each state's statutes provide guidelines for establishing when there is reasonable cause to suspect child sexual abuse and sexual maltreatment. Sexual abuse or sexual maltreatment is commonly suspected when the parent or other person legally responsible for the care of the child perpetrates the following behaviors (note that examples are not all inclusive):[9]

1. Touches a child's genitals, buttocks, breasts, or other intimate parts for the purpose of gratifying sexual desire or forces or encourages the child to touch the genitals, buttocks, breasts, or other intimate parts of the parent or legal guardian for the purpose of gratifying sexual desire.

2. Engages or attempts to engage the child in sexual intercourse or deviant sexual intercourse (for example, contact between penis and anus, mouth and penis, or mouth and vulva).

3. Forces, encourages, or willfully and / or knowingly allows a child to engage in sexual activity (such as prostitution) with other children or adults.

4. Uses a child or permits a child to be used in a sexual performance, such as a photograph, play, motion picture, or dance, giving rise to impairment or imminent danger of impairment of the child, regardless of whether the material itself is obscene.

5. Knowingly and approvingly exposes the child to sexual activity, or exhibitionism, for the purpose of sexual stimulation or gratification of another, causing harm or imminent danger of harm.

Indicators of Sexual Abuse

There are several physical signs that, although in no way conclusive, should alert mandated reporters to the possibility of sexual abuse or maltreatment. In most cass of sexual abuse, no physical indicators are present. But their absence should not lead an advocate to doubt a child's story. The following signs are commonly indicators of sexual abuse:[10]

1. Bruises on buttocks, inner thighs, or genitals.
2. Bleeding in external genitalia, vaginal, or anal areas.
3. Swelling, pain, itching, or cuts in genital or anal areas.
4. Genital discharge, stains, or blood on underclothes or torn underclothes.
5. Difficulty in walking or sitting.
6. Veneral disease.
7. Childhood pregnancy.
8. Child's report of sexual abuse by a caretaker.

Certain behaviors may point to sexual abuse but should be cautiously relied upon. Except for a child's actual report of sexual abuse, which can have high validity,[11] these behaviors are nonspecific indicators of trauma that can be seen in children who have experienced events as varied as parental divorce or witnessing an accident or act of violence. The following are signs that the child may be reacting to some sort of stress:

1. Changes in behavior, such as loss of appetite and inability to sleep.
2. Regression to more infantile behavior like bed wetting and thumb sucking.
3. Withdrawal from usual activities.
4. Poor peer relationships.
5. Fear of a person or intense dislike at being left somewhere or with someone.
6. Unusual sexual knowledge or behavior that is inappropriate for age and development.
7. Unwillingness to change for physical education class or to shower in front of peers.
8. Difficulty in concentrating at school.
9. Aggressive or disruptive behavior, delinquency, or running away.

Responding to Suspicions of Child Sexual Abuse

Disclosure of sexual abuse usually occurs prior to the child advocate's involvement with a family.[12] However, in the event that the child advocate suspects previously unreported child sexual abuse, perhaps as a result of an interview with the child, he or she should consider how to respond to these suspicions.

When a child reports being sexually abused, either directly or indirectly, the advocate may not be sure whether to believe the child. This reaction is understandable, but it should not stop the advocate from making a report. A child's statement of sexual abuse is sufficient to give reasonable cause to suspect child maltreatment. The responsibility for determining the truth of the child's statements belongs to child protective services. Experienced treatment professionals indicate that a child's statement about being sexually abused is almost always true; children generally do not lie or hallucinate about being sexually abused.[13]

Very young victims of sexual abuse tend to possess a level of detailed knowledge about sexual practices beyond the norm for their age; their sexual awareness is age inappropriate. Sexually provocative mannerisms in young children are an example of age-inappropriate behavior. Such young children, and their reports of sexual abuse, should not be dismissed when they act in sexually provocative ways.

Questions for the Advocate

It is important to learn about the alleged abusive situation. The following are fact-gathering questions that may be helpful to advocates in assessing the situation, determining where to probe further, and advocating for the child most persuasively. The advocate may obtain the answers to these questions from a variety of sources—the child, the nonabusing spouse or caretaker, the abusing spouse or caretaker, other children or relatives, police, and the protective services worker. Child sexual abuse victims are particularly vulnerable to repeated questioning about the abusive incidents by police, prosecutors, social workers, evaluators, and others. Child advocates must take special care not to increase the child's trauma by becoming just one more person who appears to doubt the child's original disclosure or who requires that she or he recount (and relive) it one more time. Advocates may be able to shield the child from multiple interviews by arranging for videotaped interviews by a qualified interviewer.

- What event, or incident of sexual abuse, has led to the present legal action? Understand the specific details of the alleged abuse. Did the abuse involve groping, inappropriate comments, and/or sexual intercourse? Where was the child touched? by whom? by what part of the alleged perpetrator's body? in what manner? Did actual physical violence or threats of physical violence accompany the sexual abuse?
- When did the incident occur? (Young children may have trouble remembering when the incident occurred because of their undeveloped sense of time. Their difficulty should not be interpreted as evidence that the abuse did not occur.)
- Who reported the incident? What were the circumstances surrounding the report? To whom was it reported?
- How soon after the incident occurred was it actually reported?
- Where has the child been living since the report was made? Where has the abuser been living?
- Who is the abuser, and what is that person's relationship to the child? What is the child's perception of their relationship? How strongly attached to the abuser is the child?
- Where did the abuse take place?
- Has the abuser been accused of abuse previously? An abuser who has already been reported for abuse will likely be relatively resistant to change.)
- Has this child been abused on other occasions by the abuser? When did the abuser first molest this child?
- Is there physical evidence of sexual abuse?
- Is the family, especially the abuser, willing to undergo treatment?

Notes

1. Faller, *Child Sexual Abuse: An Interdisciplinary Manual for Diagnosis, Case Management, and Treatment* (New York: Columbia University Press, 1988), P. 131.

2. American Humane Association, *Highlights of Official Child Neglect and Abuse Reporting 1982,* Denver: American Humane Assoc. 1984.

3. American Humane Association, *Highlights of Official Child Neglect and Abuse Reporting 1982,* Denver: American Humane Assoc. 1986.

4. D. Finkelhor, *Sexually Victimized Children* (New York: Free Press, 1979).

5. Faller, *Child Sexual Abuse,* P. 89.

6. Ibid.; Finkelhor, *Sexually Victimized Children.*

7. *For example, Finkelhor, Sexually Victimized Children,* describes four preconditions for sexual abuse and explains each on an individual and sociocultural level.

8. Ibid.

9. New York Department of Health and Department of Social Services, "Guidelines for Reporting Sexual Abuse and Maltreatment of Children," in *Official Guidelines of the State of New York Department of Health and Department of Social Services* (Albany: 1986).

10. Ibid.

11. Faller, "Is the Child Victim of Sexual Abuse Telling the Truth?" *Child Abuse and Neglect: The International Journal* 8(4) (1984): 473–481; Mary de Young, "Judging the Truthfulness of a Young Child's Allegations of Sexual Abuse," *American Journal of Orthopsychiatry* 56 (1986): 550.

12. The material in this section is from a document prepared by New York City's Special Services for Children and the Mayor's Task Force on Child Abuse and Neglect as part of a child protective training program for Preventive Service Agencies.

13. See Faller, *Child Sexual Abuse* and de Young, "Judging the Truthfulness."

15
Child Neglect

Mary, the mother of Carrie, 2 and ½ years of age and Jane, 8 months old, residing in this county and legally responsible for these children did neglect them by allowing Carrie to be left unsupervised and playing outside for five hours while she, Mary, was sleeping and having a filthy house with very little food for the children.

Children were alone all day. Neighbors called police. Neighbors state that the mother parties all night long, and the children are alone all night, and then she sleeps all day, and they are alone. The older child plays out in the street all the time. Also, there was no food at all in the house except for two frozen packages.[1]

Definition

Child neglect is a difficult condition for the advocate to identify. Many state statutes give the juvenile or family court jurisdiction over "neglect" without defining the term. "Child neglect" is often in the eye of the beholder or, like pornography, although we cannot define it, we know it when we see it. One author has called abuse and neglect of children "the sum of [a] society's actions, beliefs, and values that impede the healthy development of its children."[2]

Abuse and neglect may stem from a variety of values, beliefs, and practices, including those of the society as a whole, the institutions within that society (including the foster care and legal systems), nonrelated individuals, and families. But where abuse may leave observable signs in the physical condition of the child, neglect frequently does not. Typical cases of family neglect may involve parents or caretakers who have difficulty maintaining adequate employment, housing, and/or medical care. There may be health problems in the family, poor money management, alcohol and drug abuse, and frequent crises that require emergency

This chapter was written by Martha W. Steketee and Meryl Berlin.

services. The children, as a result, may be "neglected" through poor supervision, inadequate clothing and food, lack of medical attention, and/or care that does not encourage emotional or intellectual growth.

Societal and institutional neglect provide an important context in which to understand the neglect of children that occurs in families. Indicators of societal neglect include general conditions such as social and econonic inequality and our high societal tolerance for violence. Examples of institutional neglect include the often poor condition of foster homes and other institutions for children and the often slow and sometimes uninformed decision-making processes involving children at risk of harm and those who have been harmed by their caretakers. One of the advocate's roles is to ensure that institutional neglect of the child client does not replace family neglect. The advocate can help prevent such institutional neglect by demanding prompt decision making and individual accountability for the care of children.

Family neglect refers to the mistreatment of children by their own families, especially by primary caretakers. Just as societal neglect stems from fundamental values as to what constitutes the "good" society or the "good" adult and what type of child rearing will produce them, these values strongly shape what will be seen as neglect of children's needs in particular cases of family action or inaction. In the abstract, family neglect presents special definitional and practice problems for the legal and helping professions due to the special relationships between child and parent and between the family and the state. In application, however, neglect is defined by state statutes that may provide for medical, educational, physical, and/or emotional neglect. Advocates should be trained in the specifics of their own state's neglect statutes and should be familiar with local interpretation of these provisions by social service workers, the legal community, and the local court.

In abuse and neglect cases, advocates may encounter a medical diagnosis called "failure to thrive." This diagnosis is assigned to infants with weight gains that are disproportionately slow in comparison to gains in height and head circumference. It is generally diagnosed within the first three years of life. An organic (or physical) explanation can be found for poor weight gain in approximately 18 to 30 percent of the cases. Parental neglecet is identified as the cause of failure to thrive in another 50 percent of the cases.[3] Diagnostically, these are identified as cases of non organic failure to thrive. In these cases, for example, feeding difficulties are thought to reflect problems in the relationship between the caregiver and the infant. Generally weight gain in the hospital in response to trial feedings is taken as confirmation of this diagnosis, although not everyone accepts this view.[4]

Failure-to-thrive infants often appear sickly and socially unresponsive. Not infrequently, they suffer from other physical illnesses or from feeding problems. While advocates should not expect to assign a diagnosis themselves (this must be done by a physician), they should keep in mind that a young child's emotional distress frequently is expressed in physical ways. Thus the salient factors in the case may appear to be the child's medical status, but emotional and environmental factors may also be critical in developing an effective case plan. If the diagnosis of failure to thrive has already been assigned to a particular case, the advocate should note the measures that have been taken to assess or address problems in the relationship between the caregiver and infant. If the diagnosis has not been assigned but the condition is suspected, the advocate should consider a medical evaluation and an evaluation of the caregiver-infant relationships.

Questions for the Advocate

Current Situation

- How does the child appear? (tired? inattentive? ill?) Remember that court proceedings are frightening to most children, and this fact will affect how the child behaves with and responds to the advocate.
- Is the caretaker present at the proceedings? If so, how does the caretaker appear? If not, what is the explanation for his or her absence?
- Are other family members present at the proceedings? Do they have knowledge of the event(s) or situation(s) that brought this case to court?

Family Situation

- Where does the child live? with whom? in what neighborhood? How many children live in the home?
- Who is the primary caretaker? What relation has the caretaker to the child? If the caretaker is not the child's parents, where are the parents?
- How long has this person been the primary caretaker?
- Is the child safe in his or her current living situation?
- What other family members are available as possible temporary caretakers for the child?

Petition

- What kind of neglect has been charged? (environmental, caretaking-custodial, emotional, educational)?
- Who filed the petition?
- Who made the original charge of neglect?
- Is neglect coupled with any other charges?
- What precipitating event or situation brought this charge.
- Is this event or situation recurrent?

- To what extent does the omission reflect a lack of concern for the child, and to what extent is it a matter of social or economic conditions? For example, different case planning for the child and the family is indicated when a parent is unable to pay for or get access to needed medical care versus parents who simply fail to bring the child to medical appointments covered by insurance or government benefits.

- If the report includes a reference like "mom runs the streets" or "is unresponsive to treatment," what precisely does the petitioner mean?

- Does this family, parent, or child have a case history with the court or social service agencies? Do the prior charges or incidents seem to have any relevance to the present proceedings?

Notes

1. The excerpts are from a juvenile court petition. The names have been changed.

2. J.M. Giovannoni, "Child Abuse and Neglect," in J. Laird and A. Hartman, eds., *A Handbook of Child Welfare: Context, Knowledge, and Practice* (New York: Free Press, 1985), P. 194.

3. D.C. Bross and L.F. Michaels, Eds., *Foundations of Child Advocacy: Legal Representation of the Maltreated Child* (Longment, Colo.: Bookmakers Guild, 1987, P. 39.

4. M. Kotelchuck, "Non-Organic Failure-to-Thrive: The Status of Interactional and Environmental Etiologic Theories," in B.W. Camp, ed., *Advances in Behavioral Pediatrics*, vol. 1 (Greenwich, Conn.,: JAI Press, 1980), pp. 29–51.

16
Skills in Mediation and Negotiation

The child advocate can play a significant role as a mediator. He or she is on neither the side of the agency nor the parents; rather the advocate speaks up for the child. The advocate need not take an adversarial position on either side. In fact, the interests of the child are often served by voluntary resolution of the legal dispute, thus avoiding contested trial. A contested proceeding will not only delay implementation of a case plan but will take considerably more time and put substantial additional stresses on the child and family. The child's advocate, therefore, can be a useful bridge between the agency and the parents and may be able to find terms of settlement that all parties find acceptable.

Win-Lose or Problem-solving Approach

There are many ways to approach negotiation. Much negotiation that we engage in is adversarial: if you win, I lose; therefore I want to win more than I want to lose, and I want you to lose more than you win. It is competitive. The implications of that win-lose mentality is that you keep your cards close to your chest. You have a strategy of negotiation, and you know what your resistant points are going to be. There are timing ploys; if you are going to give something, you want the other side to give something. You identify leverage points. The win-lose mentality, which characterizes most of what lawyers do, is a power struggle.

To get to a problem-solving situation, the parties have to recognize that the shortcoming of the win-lose approach is that it is not cooperative and it tends to restrict rather than expand choices. A problem-solving approach requires a supportive, nondefensive climate—one of acceptance and trust. We need the expectation that in juvenile court child protection proceedings, there is going to be a different way to approach problems.

Approaching a case in a problem-solving way requires engaging in some joint fact finding. Sometimes the social workers misjudge the case and do not have the facts right. It is not uncommon that the parents have not given exactly the straight story. The advocate will talk to all the parties and between the story of the social worker and the story of the parents will get the facts straight.

The advocate, and the other participants in the process, should set forth as many solutions or alternatives to the presenting problems as they possibly can. A range of options should be defined. The more options there are, the more likely it is that the participants will find a solution to the problem that is acceptable to both family and the agency and still protect the child.

Ideally the advocate should include everyone on all the teams in this process; the lawyer representing the agency, the caseworker, and the parents and their attorney. Unless everyone participates in this process, someone may be left behind and end up killing a settlement the others were moving toward. The advocate must be alert to avoid stalemate.

Negotiating at Every Stage of the Court Process

Just as the social worker has negotiated with the family prior to invoking the power of the court, the negotiating process should continue through all the formal phases of the court proceedings. The social worker should recognize that contested court proceedings are costly to the child and family. The relationship between agency and parents becomes, at least for a time, adversarial. Resolution of contested cases is time-consuming for all concerned. The treatment goals for the child and family are not usually furthered while the court action is pending. In many cases, the negative effects of adversarial court action may be reduced by a negotiated resolution.

The advocate must not give up too quickly. Often discussions that occur early in a child protection case are unsuccessful. The process has a way of bringing parties together who start out apart. Advocates must not fall into the mind-set that trying to settle the case once means they should not try again later. Agreement may be reached on some issues at every stage of the court process. Sometimes a case that starts with a particularly adversarial and distrustful tone evolves into a cooperative and trusting relationship. Advocates should be realistic and not expect miracles, but they can keep working on developing a cooperative, problem-solving approach.

Predicting the Outcome

Professionals regularly involved in the court process can generally predict with some accuracy what the court is likely to do given the strength of each side's legal case and the reasonableness of each side's position. In the process of negotiation, information is shared in a persuasive fashion so as to convince the other side of the strength and reasonableness of one's position and the likelihood that the court will rule in that way anyway. One assesses the case of the opponent and in the light of that assessment modifies one's position if the case is found to be weak or not reasonable or if the other side's proposals are acceptable alternatives. By a process of mutual give and take, some prediction is made by each side as to what the court is likely to do after full hearing. Negotiation is an opportunity to agree to a resolution of the problem that is close to what the court would order if a contested and adversarial trial were to take place.

If the assessments of the strengths and weaknesses of the cases differ, no negotiated settlement will result. In addition certain elements of each case, such as the safety of the child, will be nonnegotiable always. The process of give and take, of assessing one's own case and the case of an opponent, can become quite complicated and occur over several meetings.

Flexibility: The Search for Positive Solutions

Four major issues are negotiated in child protection cases:

1. Jurisdiction.
2. Placement of the children. This is often the most important issue to the parents. They may not care so much about the abstract notion of court jurisdiction; they want their child home tonight.
3. Visits.
4. The treatment plan. The advocate should not abrogate the treatment plan to caseworkers alone. As good as caseworkers might be, they are not as good as we would like them to be. Advocates need to critique casework plans carefully and arrive at creative alternatives. Coming up with alternatives is the basic element of successful negotiation—where all parties can be winners.

Preparation is 80 percent of a good trial. Preparation is equally important for negotiation. Each of the dimensions of child advocacy leads up to the mediation and problem-solving stage. The advocate wants to have completed an investigation so he or she knows the facts as well as possible. He or she wants to have consulted all the persons interested in the procedure, asking, "What do you think the problems are?" Once the problems are defined, the advocate can ask, "What do you think are the solutions to those problems? To get at those solutions, who should do what and when? How should the personal links between the child and family be made?

Even the most intractable parent may change his or her position once court action is begun. The prospect of appearing in court and the advice of a lawyer may temper a formerly uncompromising attitude. On the other hand, information not previously available to the social worker may surface that tends to alter his or her evaluation of the case. The social worker may have been mistaken as to the true facts or may have misjudged important elements of the case. Therefore, the positions of both the social worker and the parents may become fluid as the court process starts. A negotiated resolution may become possible.

Identifying Options for Mutual Gain

To negotiate effectively in the legal context, one must be keenly aware of the various options available. On the issue of whether the court should take jurisdiction of a child, independent of consideration of where the child should be placed, there are several options (presented in escalating degrees of court involvement).

- Agree not to petition the court.
- File petition.
- Agree to withdraw a petition already filed or to recommend dismissal by the court.
- Amend the petition to add or delete allegations.
- Adjourn.
- Parents plea no contest.
- Parents admit allegations of petition.
- Parents deny allegations of petition; trial date set.

Custody of the child(ren) is generally paramount to the parents. The following negotiating options are available:

- Return the child home immediately.
- Return the child home soon (on the condition that . . .).
- Return the child on a date certain (on the condition that . . .).
- Arrange visitation daily, weekly, overnight, weekends, supervised or unsupervised, depending on the child's needs. Visitation arrangements may be conditioned on parents actions of one sort or another.
- Place the child in a home requested by the parents, such as the home of a relative or licenseable friend of the family.

Certain elements of a treatment plan that the social worker considers desirable may be particularly onerous to the parents. The advocate needs to identify them and attempt to fashion a treatment plan most likely to be accepted by the family. Perhaps an element of a plan that is especially distasteful to the family can be bargained away in exchange for their agreement to accept court jurisdiction and a dispositional order that will meet the family needs.

The following negotiated resolutions are possible:

Withdraw the Petition:	The parents agree to accept the service plan.
Adjourn:	The parents agree to use the time to improve conditions and correct deficiencies.
Return child to parents' custody: The child is placed in a parent-requested home, with generous visitation allowed.	The parents admit petition or plead no contest and agree to needed services ordered by the court at dispositional hearing.

Traditional Adversarial Procedures

Although child advocates may prefer a nonadversarial approach, when differences regarding the true facts or the proper responses to the family problems are irreconcilable, the adversarial system is well suited to resolve the conflict. In some cases, nothing short of court wardship and a period of foster care will adequately safeguard the child. Unless the parents are willing to admit the petition or not contest it, there may be no basis for negotiation. Similarly, the attorney for a set of parents may disagree with the allegations of the petition and the worker's assessment of the petition's strength, and his or her clients may be unwilling to consent to any form of state intervention and may have instructed him or her to contest all allegations. Here again, negotiation will not be successful. A contested hearing (trial) will likely result.

As long as all sides share a similar view of the problem and a desired outcome, such as a family reunification, a conciliation approach is likely to be successful. But when the parents, child protection agency, and child's advocate do not see the problem in the same way or differ markedly on what the state intervention ought to be on behalf of the child, some means of resolving those conflicts must be available. For example, if the parent, agency, and advocate believe that the case requires a short period of foster care for the child while the mother obtains suitable housing away from an abusive boyfriend, cooperative agreement should be possible. If, however, the focus of the agency or the advocate turns to termination of parental rights or other actions that deprive the parents of custody, or where actions are proposed to which the advocate in good conscience cannot agree on behalf of the child, traditional adversarial due process procedures are the best means of resolving the conflict and protecting the rights of all concerned. The traditional due process procedures remain available for cases in which conciliation and mediation have not worked. The proportion of cases in which the adversarial approach is relied upon may be reduced to a distinct minority however.

17
Barriers to Effective Child Advocacy

We would like to live in an ideal world, where nothing is wrong and everyone is treated fairly; where, in the event that something does go wrong, those of us who are in a position to intercede on behalf of injured parties do so quickly and cooperatively. We do not live in a world like this. People are treated unkindly and unfairly. Furthermore, those who seek to intercede are not always unified in their efforts to help others. Antagonisms exist, and agendas differ.

All agree that children ought not to suffer. However, parents are not always able to provide their children with a healthy or nurturing environment in which to develop. Child protective services and the judicial system have attempted to respond to this problem by nudging parents toward more responsible parenting behaviors. Ideally the system should effectively work toward that end. Because it does not, advocates for children, including lawyers and programs for CASAs, have attempted to step into the gap. These advocates have taken on the task of playing watchdog to an overloaded system on behalf of the child. Child advocates work to ensure that it is indeed the children's best interests and not expediency that is served during the judicial proceedings.

The child advocate must act as the child's mouthpiece and ensure that the child's best interests are served. But a variety of external and internal barriers work against the advocates in the pursuit of their duties. The advocate may experience personal barriers, information barriers, and systemic barriers.

Personal Barriers

The Place of Personal Values

Personal biases can play a role in the decision-making process through which advocates' recommendations of what is in the best interests of the child must

---

This chapter was written by Liese A. Hull.

come. In practice, advocates may often speak and act as if the best interests of a child were self-evident, tacitly assuming that their judgments are shared, at least by all "sensitive" or "moral" people. Yet from any examination of the basis for decisions about what indeed are the best interests of children, it is clear that they often stem from highly personal life experiences: the kinds of family relationships advocates knew as children; the moral values they adopted at an early age concerning violence, authority, autonomy, compassion, and so on. It is important for child advocates to reflect on the orgins of these values, so that they may act with a clearer sense of why they make their judgments and with an appreciation that values and judgments arise from a special set of circumstances, not from some universal truth.

Two different kinds of attitudes, presumably, could stem from one's own family experience. One might view that experience as a norm or an ideal that constitutes an implicit standard against which other families are judged. Alternatively, one might consciously or unconsciously reject some or all of that experience and hold its opposite as one's standard. In either case, the advocate's view may be disproportionately driven by personal experience that could bias his or her judgment of the issues faced in this role. For example, if the child's representative comes from a family where there was physical or emotional abuse, such an experience might predispose him or her to overidentify with a child whose case might seem superficially similar to the advocate's own history, though the objective circumstances might argue otherwise. Advocates should try to recognize when these biases may be operating, and avoid letting them drive their decision making. The following case illustrates the issue.

> A baby diagnosed as failure to thrive has been brought before the court referee. He is twenty months old, rather small for his age, looks sickly, and is unresponsive in general. An informal child care arrangement has been worked out within the family system. The baby is usually cared for by his maternal step-grandmother, the middle child (a three-year-old girl) is cared for by the paternal grandparents, and the oldest child (a five-year-old boy) is usually in the care of the father. The mother rarely, if ever, has direct and sole responsibility of all three of her children at once.
>
> The case is before the referee because the mother has failed to keep an appointment for a diagnostic test scheduled for the youngest child (the failure-to-thrive baby). The mom has a history of "disappearing" at inopportune times, and this behavior was considered inappropriate in the light of the medical difficulties that the child is experiencing.

Without adding further details at this time, we will use what we know about the case thus far to explore how individual biases can affect decision making. If we subscribe to the notion of family as nuclear family only (indeed the judge who presided over the dispositional hearing in this case clearly indicated that this was the model he held dear), then the family system described probably seems somewhat dysfunctional. The parents, who are either incapable of or reluctant to provide primary care for their entire enclave of children are not properly fulfilling their role as parents.

If, however, our definition of family allows for greater functional variety, where the responsibilities of child rearing can be shared by extended family members and still be considered just as valid as in an intact nuclear family, then the family arrangement outlined in the case example may not seem dysfunctional. In fact, the parents could be commended for the consideration they have show their children seeking out and setting up an alternative mechanism for the nurture and care of their children rather than risking the possibility of their abuse or neglect as an outcome of the parents' feeling overburdened.

Some ethnic groups typically use the resources of the extended family in child rearing more frequently than those who subscribe to more mainstream cultural dictates. Among these peoples, joint child rearing is not considered dysfunctional or an indication that the parents are shirking their duties but an admission by the parents that they need help. It is a viable alternative that may often operate in the best interests of the child.

That we are wedded to our value system is a fact. Our biases are activated when elements in our environment actively or passively challenge that value system. Biases act to confirm the principles by which we conduct our lives. That is fine for us; however, we must recognize that something that is functional for us in our environment may not be functional for a family that lives in a different environment, comes from a different culture, or exists within a different economic class.

In the case scenario, the temptation to opt for removal, not just of the youngest child but the others also, or to push for reunification of the siblings under a common roof, was there. Because the protective services (PS) worker on this case had a history of dealing with the family, she was enlightened enough about the family ecology to see that, apart from the mother's disturbing pattern of disappearing, this was not necessarily a dysfunctional family system. The worker merely requested that legal authority for care of the infant be given to the maternal step-grandmother. This woman was more capable than the baby's mother of offering consistent care both physiologically and psychosocially to the sick infant.

Personal Biases

It would be naive to suggest that decisions can be made in a vacuum, separate from the attitudes and values that have influenced the individual's choices made throughout life. But all advocates must become aware of all of the elements that go into one's decision making. Once these elements are clear, advocates can work to weed out the logical decision making from the gut reaction. Should the advocate suggest that the referee authorize a petition that suggests removal of the child because the advocate is horrified and cannot imagine a child surviving in circumstances that are alien to his or her own upbringing? Does the advocate believe that the child's life is at risk in these circumstances because there is real and imminent danger in his or her present home? These are two separate issues. The first is driven by subjective feeling, the second by an objective assessment of the information gathered from the petition and the participants in the case.

Getting in touch with why we come to certain decisions requires us to become aware of the elements that comprise the decision-making process we employ. You may want to walk through, step by step, how you arrive at a decision, writing down all the thoughts that cross your mind as you reach a conclusion. Then go back and review them, separating those based on subjective reaction from those based on objective fact. If subjective feeling is overriding objective fact, you may want to work to change this pattern. You also will want to guard against its influence when you are participating on a case—perhaps by consulting with others.

Informational Barriers

The processes of investigation, consultation, and problem solving, along with the advocate's formal training, will reap a substantial body of information for the advocate's use. Nevertheless, each case will raise unique issues, some of which the advocate may not immediately recognize. Generally information barriers exist of two types: personal barriers and systematic barriers.

Personal Information Barriers

For lay advocates, one typical personal information barrier is the lack of detailed knowledge about the legal aspects of child protection. For example, in the case discussed, the protective services worker, who had been observing this family system since the onset of the failure-to-thrive diagnosis, recommended full-time placement of the child with the maternal step-grandmother in order to ensure that medical care could be obtained on a consistent basis for the child. After talking with the mother and other relatives, it became apparent that placing the child away from the mother with its maternal step-grandmother who was a familiar person would probably not hurt this child. The maternal step-grandmother indicated a willingness to care for him despite his condition and indicated also that she had done so off and on for most of his life anyway. In actuality, the hearing would simply legalize an already-existing arrangement within the family system.

Someone without legal training would not realize that the law of this state does not allow the court to order that a child be placed in an unlicensed, unrelated home. Legally this placement arrangement could not be approved without the permission of the parents; the maternal step-grandmother was not a blood relative (she had formerly been married to the mother's father), nor was she a licensed foster care provider. Fortunately, both parents were present at the hearing and were willing to enter a plea to the charges in the petition and actively assent to the placement of the child in the care of the step-grandmother. Otherwise this placement recommendation could not have been legally affirmed.

Why was it considered important that the child be kept within the family ecosystem? The placement was recommended to ensure continuity of care for the sake of the baby. This was important because the child was diagnosed as failure to thrive. This raises another component of the informational barrier issue. Lack of knowledge about the types of child maltreatment, theories about the causes of maltreatment, typical professional responses to each type represent another critical information barrier, which arises most frequently before the advocate has had substantial case experience. The case can illustrate this point.

The baby in the example was diagnosed as having failure to thrive. What is failure to thrive? Although there are physical manifestations of failure to thrive, it is regarded as a condition that arises due to nonorganic or nonphysiological causes, including an infant's being raised in a nonnurturing environment.

What is an appropriate case plan in the face of a diagnosis of failure to thrive? That is, what is an appropriate placement, and what services are needed? While failure-to-thrive children certainly need consistent medical attention, the day-to-day care of the child should be characterized by a loving, secure, and consistent environment. The daily care of the child is equally critical, and without such a placement, the condition will continue. With it, the baby may begin to thrive.

In the example, the social worker recommended that the maternal step-grandmother be given legal authority over the child in order to ensure consistent medical care. Making recommendations for medical services, though important, does not fully address the child's needs, however. The quality of care the child will receive from the step-grandmother is equally important. Direct intervention with the grandmother, possibly by the caseworker, a public health nurse, or an infant mental health specialist, can ensure that the grandmother understands the special needs of the child and is able to provide consistency and nurture.

What is failure to thrive? What is considered sexual abuse? neglect? It is not necessarily just knowing the particular terminology that is of concern but realizing that one's recommendations must address the conditions that have befallen the child. What is an appropriate recommendation in the face of a diagnosis of failure to thrive? What kinds of other relevant considerations should we be aware of? What kind of services does this imply are necessary for the child?

Finding the Information

In all likelihood an advocate will serve a relatively short tenure—probably a year, not more than two at any one time. It is impossible to squeeze legal, social work, psychological, and medical training into the preparation that potential advocates receive. Therefore we suggest that child advocacy programs be organized so that in addition to regular supervision, legal, social work, and medical consultation are available as needed.

In addition, one important skill to acquire and utilize is that of networking. Making links with lawyers, protective service workers, psychologists, and medical professionals from throughout your community will provide access to an important body of knowledge. The advocate should seek to become acquainted with a number of professionals, sampling here and there in order to edify himself or herself enough to make informed decisions that work toward the interests of the children being served.

In summary, there are three critical personal information barriers:

1. Knowledge about legal process and placement options: What defines a legal placement? Are there out-of-home placement options that do not require juvenile court supervision (guardianships, power of attorney, informal parental agreements for short periods of time)? How does one negotiate such a placement?

2. Familiarity with the type of abuse or neglect the child has suffered (such as failure to thrive, sexual abuse, neglect, and abandonment) and the differential influences these conditions exert on placement and treatment decisions (for example, when is it better to look for placement outside the family system?)

3. Obtaining the information and background necessary to make more informed decisions: What professionals should the advocate link up with and how?

Systemic Barriers

Caseworker Overload

The last type of barrier we will address is one that exists in the advocate's interactions with other champions of children. At times the antagonism that can exist when the advocate is trying to do his or her job is quite difficult to understand.

Before going to court, there is bound to be apprehension about the way parents and children will receive the advocate. It is distressing that one must add to that apprehension the realization that one might be considered a nuisance by some protective service workers and some court workers. Part of the resentment may exist because it is likely that the advocate's recommendations will require the social services worker to do more work than he or she feels there is time for. Since caseloads are generally heavy and most social service agencies work on a crisis orientation, thoroughly and quickly following up a case plan may not be their standard procedure. Since the advocate is perceived as creating more work for an already overburdened caseworker, the advocate at times may be the target of antagonism.

It would be helpful to all concerned parties if the advocate keeps in mind that court workers and protective services workers are under a lot of pressure. Often the antagonism arises because advocates' recommendations are perceived as judgmental and critical. Fostering a good working relationship with social workers based on respect and commonality of purpose will ease some of the inevitable tensions.

Overlapping Jurisdictions of Agencies and Courts.

In most states, publicly funded services for children and families are categorial programs; that is, the family must meet certain eligibility criteria before services are available. Typically these criteria include family composition (for example, a single mother with a dependent child), income guidelines, or diagnosis of illness or handicap (mental health services may be available only where there is a diagnosis of mental illness or deficiency). This may mean that the services that a child is eligible to receive could be determined by who is paying for the foster care facility he or she is placed in—county, state, or federal government; public child welfare, mental health, or the medical care system.

In addition, juvenile courts in many states continue to provide protective, foster care, and treatment services alongside federally and state-funded social services departments. This may mean, for example, that the family's caseworker may be changed in the middle of a sensitive stage of the case development, requiring the advocate to work not only with new personnel but with a different system of service delivery. In some cases, two caseworkers may be assigned to the same case.

Further, a family accused of abusing a child may be involved in several different courts at the same time. In Michigan, for example, a troubled family could be involved in simultaneous proceedings in circuit court concerning a divorce child custody dispute; probate court concerning a guardianship; juvenile court, concerning civil child protecton proceedings; and circuit or district court for criminal prosecution on the same charges of abuse. Each of these courts has the power to make certain orders affecting the child's welfare, including incarceration of the parent, custody of the child, or treatment for the parents. Even seasoned lawyers get mired in such confusion of jurisdiction and responsibility.

Advocates need not master every system in order to provide effective advocacy for the child. They need to know whether certain services they perceive as necessary will be available when placement arrangements are made. By asking the right questions, as early as they seem appropriate, their decisions will be more informed.

Dealing with Difference of Agenda

By necessity, since the advocate's interest is primarily on behalf of the child and the protective services worker is dealing with the family as a whole, the agendas with which each walks into the preliminary hearing may be quite different. For instance, the protective services worker could be using the petition to coerce a resistant parent into a drug screening and counseling program, without being focused on what might be in the child's best interests. The worker also has a large caseload with limited time and resources to be spread over all of his or her clients. An advocate usually has only a few clients at a time for whom he or she wants the very best of care. These are only some of the potential sources of antagonism between the child advocate and the other participants in the child protection process.

Who Are the Real Child Advocates Anyway?

Nearly all of the actors engaged in the child protection process view themselves as child advocates. Advocates who represent the child cannot afford to be self-righteous; they are well advised to begin from a premise of mutual respect for others with whom they will have to deal. They should attempt to build bridges of cooperation so others view them as members of the same team working on behalf of the children. Ideally all in this process will see that mutual cooperation will lead to the best outcome for the most important figure in this drama, the child.

Epilogue

T he material in this book is to be used as a resource in concert with other resources; it is not meant to stand on its own. It does not contain the last word on the process or the concept of advocacy but is, rather, a starting point. We hope to have provided an on-the-job reference out of which much more work will grow from several different perspectives. It must be clearly understood and remembered, however, that the knowledge, information, and skills necessary to be a good child advocate require more than we have presented. The quest for excellence as a child advocate begins but does not end here.

We assume that each jurisdiction's definition of child abuse and neglect will be incorporated into the training and preparation advocates receive. Because statutes and practices differ from place to place, we cannot offer a single definition. Working definitions of child abuse, neglect, and sexual abuse will come after examining state statutes, case law, and the current practices of the local courts and social agencies. We hope that advocates will appreciate the cultural relativity and subjectivity of the concept of child maltreatment and always bear in mind the role that personal bias may play in the way information is absorbed and processed.

Advocates' sleuthing abilities may be tested somewhat when they attempt to discover the availability of services for children and families. But they will become familiar with those services that are available and pass that knowledge and experience on to others. Gaps in services should be pointed out to other advocates and responsible professionals, policymakers, and politicians.

Patience and persistence characterize the best advocates—for the individual child and for a class of children. Those same skills will aid advocates' efforts to stay on top of case follow-up activities. Follow-up is one of the easiest dimensions to neglect yet one of the most important for the advocate to do.

Although we have spent much time and effort developing this concept of child advocates, ours is certainly not the only definition. This book does not

---

The Epilogue was written by Liese A. Hull.

purport to offer the final word on how to think and act as an advocate. We hope it invites all advocates to think of the broad boundaries of the role and of the wealth of available information that can help make wise decisions on behalf of children.

We hope this material, along with on-site training, can set countless advocates on their way to effective advocacy for abused and neglected children. In the end, however, experience is the best teacher. Nothing will be as crucial in sharpening skills and exposing gaps in knowledge as will actual cases. We share the excitement as child advocates everywhere take on their new challenge!

Appendix A: Proposal for Legislation Establishing a Statewide Child Advocacy Office and Setting Standards for Representing the Child

I. Purpose

The purpose of this statute is to facilitate the establishment of CASA [court-appointed special advocate] programs in counties throughout the state and to establish statewide standards for any person appointed to represent the interests of the child in a child protection proceeding.

Author's note: Although state law requires that children be independently represented in child protection proceedings, there is no clear description of the role and duties of a child advocate. It is our hope that articulating a minimum standard for child advocates and engaging the community in child advocacy will increase the effectiveness of the representation children receive in child protective proceedings.

II. Definitions

"Child's Advocate means (a) a child's attorney appointed by the probate court and (b) a CASA appointed by the probate court.

This proposal was prepared by the University of Michigan Child Advocacy Fellowship in 1988–1989, supported by the National Center for Child Abuse and Neglect, which provides the University of Michigan and nine other universities with funding for interdisciplinary training programs in child abuse and neglect.

This proposal reflects the work of Anne E. Read, law fellow; Mary Elizabeth Pratt, law fellow; Matt Mendel, clinical psychology fellow; Myrna Kleis-Miller, social work fellow; Professor Sallie R.Churchill, School of Social Work; and Professor Donald N. Duquette, Law School.

"Coordinator" means a person selected by a local director to assist in the administration of the program.

"Court Appointed Special Advocate (CASA)" means a trained community volunteer qualified under the terms of this Act to be appointed by the probate court to represent the interests of a child subject to child protection proceedings.

"Interdisciplinary" means including professionals and others from fields such as education, law, medicine, psychology, and social work who have demonstrated an interest in children and their welfare.

"Local" means a county or a multicounty region which has voluntarily joined together to form a local board.

"Local Board" means the local body charged with implementing a child advocacy program on the local level consistent with state law and the policies of the State Child Advocacy Board.

"Local Director" means the director appointed by the local board to administer the local child advocacy program.

"Staff Attorney" means an attorney selected by the local director to assist CASAs. The staff attorney may serve as the attorney for the child if so appointed by the probate court.

"State Administrator" means the administrator of the State Child Advocacy Office who is appointed by the State Child Advocacy Board.

"State Child Advocacy Board" means the body charged with setting policy and overseeing the operation of the State Child Advocacy Office.

III. Organization–State

A. The State Child Advocacy Board

(1) **Appointment.** The State Child Advocacy Board shall be administratively located in the State Court Administrator's Office. The initial appointments to the State Child Advocacy Board shall be made by the State Supreme Court within 90 days of the effective date of this Act. Three of the initial appointments shall be for a term of one year, three shall be for a term of two years, and three shall be for a term of three years. All members appointed thereafter shall serve for three-year terms. The State Child Advocacy Board shall be responsible for appointing members to replace those members whose terms have expired.

(2) **Composition.** The State Child Advocacy Board shall consist of nine members. State Child Advocacy Board members shall represent an interdisciplinary and geographic cross-section of the state.

(3) **Duties.** The State Child Advocacy Board shall:

(a) Appoint the state administrator.

(b) Make initial appointments to local boards.

(c) Review the rules establishing criteria for local boards' eligibility for state funds as proposed by the state administrator. The State Child Advocacy Board shall promulgate the final rules within 90 days of the appointment of the state administrator.

(d) Evaluate the performance of the state administrator.

(e) Review the state administrator's evaluation of the effectiveness of local CASA programs.

(f) Identify future needs of state and local child advocacy programs.

(g) Develop policies that facilitate the creation and increase the efficacy of local CASA programs.

(h) Monitor and evaluate state child welfare services and identify to the legislature needs for improved services.

B. State Administrator

(1) **Appointment.** The state administrator will be appointed by the State Child Advocacy Board.

(2) **Qualifications.** The state administrator should have experience in both law and social work and have demonstrated an interest in children and their welfare.

(3) **Duties.** The state administrator shall:

(a) Comply with the requirements of this Act and the policy decisions of the State Child Advocacy Board.

(b) Propose rules to the State Child Advocacy Board establishing criteria for local boards' eligibility for state funds.

(c) Consult with local groups interested in starting a CASA program.

(d) Review applications by new and existing CASA programs and determine whether they qualify for state funds.

(e) Distribute funds to those programs which qualify for state funds.

(f) Develop a CASA training manual and training program.

(g) Approve local CASA training programs.

(h) Evaluate the effectiveness of local CASA programs and report to the State Child Advocacy Board.

IV. Organization—Local

A. Local Board

(1) **Appointment.** The State Child Advocacy Board shall make initial appointments to local boards. Three of the initial appointments shall be for a term of one year, three shall be for a term of two years, and three shall be for a term of three years. All members appointed thereafter shall serve for one-year terms. The local board shall be responsible for appointing members to replace those members whose terms have expired.

(2) **Composition.** The local board shall consist of nine members. At all times, at least one member of the local board shall be a probate court judge or his/her designee. Local board members shall represent an interdisciplinary cross-section of the community.

(3) **Duties.** The local board shall:

(a) Appoint a local director and evaluate the director's performance.
(b) Promote effective relationships between the CASA program and the probate court, local agencies and the community.
(c) Cooperate with State Child Advocacy Board efforts to lobby for necessary resources and services for children.
(d) Raise funds to supplement allocated state funds.
(e) Create policy for operation of local CASA programs consistent with state law and policy.

B. Local Director

(a) **Appointment.** The local board shall appoint a local director to the CASA Program.

(2) **Qualifications.** The local director should have training and experience in child development and permanency planning for children. The local director should be familiar with the probate court, child welfare agencies, and other resources available in the community.

(3) **Duties.** The local director shall be responsible for applying for state and local funds for which the local program may be eligible and administering the local CASA program. The local director shall:

(a) Have primary responsibility for the recruitment, selection, training, supervision and dismissal of CASAs. The local director shall actively recruit CASAs from diverse socioeconomic backgrounds to adequately represent a cross-section of the community. The local director shall make the final determination regarding a volunteer's participation in the program.

(b) Appoint staff attorneys as needed.

(c) Appoint and supervise coordinators and clerical staff as required by the size of the program.

(d) Supplement the state training manual and program with local rules and practices as necessary.

(e) Assign CASAs to particular cases as they are referred from the probate court. The local director shall assign a CASA to a case according to the CASA's expressed wishes, qualifications, case load, and availability.

C. *Coordinators*

(1) **Appointment.** Coordinators may be appointed by the local director. Coordinators may be paid staff or volunteers.

(2) **Duties.** Coordinators may aid the local director by:

(a) Recruiting CASAs.

(b) Conducting training and continuing education seminars for CASAs.

(c) Directly supervising CASAs.

D. *Staff Attorney*

(1) **Appointment.** The local director shall appoint at least one attorney with experience and proven interest in child welfare as staff attorney. The staff attorney or attorneys may be paid or serve as volunteers. The duties of the CASA staff attorney may also be performed by the attorney appointed by the probate court to represent the child in a particular case.

(2) **Duties.** The staff attorney shall:

(a) Provide legal consultation to CASAs.

(b) Attend hearings at which an assigned CASA requires legal assistance.

(c) Fulfill duties of the child's advocate if appointed by the probate court to represent the child.

Author's note: The establishment of local boards is designed to mobilize grass-roots support for CASA programs at the local level. In counties with preexisting CASA programs, the program staff may nominate members for the local board. Nominations must be approved by the State Child Advocacy Board.

As more fully presented in the following section, this proposal anticipates the CASA and attorney for the child working as a team on behalf of the child. Thus the local court could appoint the CASA staff attorney as attorney for the child or the attorney appointed to represent the child could fulfill the duties of the CASA staff attorney. CASAs would not function without lawyer supervision available to them.

In rare circumstances, a court might appoint an attorney for the child who would function separate from the CASA. For instance in the case of a mature child under age fourteen, the court might appoint a CASA (with the CASA staff attorney available for assistance) to represent the best interests of the child and an attorney for the child to represent the child's stated wishes.

V. CASA Volunteers: Qualifications, Training, and Supervision

A. Qualifications

A CASA volunteer shall:

(1) Be at least 21 years old.

(2) Have demonstrated an interest in child welfare.

(3) Commit to one year of service.

(4) Have transportation.

(5) Participate in interviews and consent to a criminal record check to determine their fitness for CASA responsibilities.

(6) A qualified adult shall not be discriminated against based upon age, ethnicity, marital status, race, religion, sex, sexual orientation, or socioeconomic status.

B. Training

The CASA must successfully complete a training program approved by the state administrator before assignment to a case. Thereafter, the CASA must participate in ongoing training as prescribed by the local director.

C. Supervision

The CASA serves under supervision of the local director or coordinator. It is the CASA's responsibility to confer regularly with the supervisor and to inform the supervisor of developments in the case. The CASA shall submit all recommendations and reports to the supervisor for review before submitting such reports to the probate court.

VI. Appointment and Termination

A. *Appointment*

(1) CASAs

(a) The probate court may appoint the CASA program to represent a child in child protection cases arising under state law.
(b) The local director shall assign individual CASAs to particular cases as they are referred from the probate court.
(c) The CASA shall file an appearance which shall contain a statement disclosing the existence of any interest which the CASA holds in relation to the minor, the minor's family, or any other person in the proceeding before the court or other matters.

(2) **Attorneys.** In any case in which a CASA is appointed, the probate court shall also appoint either a CASA staff attorney as the child's attorney or the child's attorney to act as legal advisor to the CASA.

B. *Termination*

The CASA's appointment to a case shall last during the pendency of the probate court's jurisdiction. A CASA may, however, be discharged from responsibility at any time by order of the probate court or by the local director who shall appoint a replacement.

Author's note: Although the appointment of the CASA program is left to the discretion of the probate court judge, the assignment of an individual CASA to a particular case would be made by the program director. Appointment of the CASA program does not satisfy the probate court's obligation to appoint an attorney for the child, although the court is encouraged to appoint the same attorney as the child's attorney and CASA staff attorney (legal advisor to the CASA). The staff attorney may concurrently represent the child and act as legal adviser to the CASA. Alternatively, if the probate judge chooses to appoint an attorney to represent the child, separate from the CASA program, a CASA may also be appointed to the case. In this event, the staff attorney would continue to act as legal adviser to the CASA.

This recommendation treats the CASA and the attorney for the child as a team in nearly all cases. The CASA will conduct the investigation, monitor compliance with the case plan and court orders, and may make recommendations to the probate court regarding services and placement based on the best interests standard. The attorney provides the CASA with consultation and direction regarding legal issues, prepares all legal documents, subpoenas witnesses, and presents the case to the probate court. This model is designed to respond to the special needs of children in abuse and neglect proceedings while respecting traditional legal safeguards.

VII. Duties of the Child's Advocate

A. The duty of the child's advocate, both CASA and child's attorney, is to represent the interests of the child. A child fourteen years of age or older is presumed capable of determining what is in his or her best interests. It is the duty of the child's advocate to represent the child's wishes in such cases. For children less than fourteen years of age, the child's advocate shall make a determination as to the best interests of the child regardless of whether that determination reflects the wishes of the child. However, the wishes of the child are always relevant to the determination of best interests and shall be weighed according to the competence and maturity of the child.

B. The child's advocate shall perform the following duties. When a child's attorney and a CASA are appointed to represent a child together, each shall be jointly and severally responsible for discharging the duties.

1) Appear at all hearings to represent competently the interests of the child in child protective proceedings brought pursuant to state law.

2) Conduct an independent investigation, including interviewing the child(ren), parents, social workers, and other persons to properly ascertain the facts and circumstances underlying the allegation that the child is a dependent or neglected child within the jurisdiction of the probate court.

3) Ascertain the interests of the child, taking into consideration the child's wishes according to the competence and maturity of the child.

4) Provide a written report of findings and recommendations to the probate court at adjudication, disposition, review hearings, permanency hearings and termination of parental rights hearings.

5) Urge that specific and clear orders are entered for evaluation, assessment, services, and treatment for the child and the child's family.

6) Monitor implementation of case plans and dispositional orders to determine whether services ordered by the probate court are actually provided, are provided in a timely manner, and are accomplishing their desired goal.

7) Inform the probate court if the services are not being made available to the child and/or family, if the family fails to take advantage of such services, or if such services are not achieving their purpose.

8) Identify the common interests among the parties and to the extent possible act as mediator to promote a cooperative resolution of the matter.

9) Consult with other professionals liberally, including program staff of the CASA program, in identifying the child's interests, current and future placements, and necessary services.

10) Advocate for the interests of the child in mental health, educational, juvenile justice, and other community systems when related to the circumstances causing the child to come within the neglect jurisdiction of the probate court.

11) Attend training programs as prescribed by the local CASA director for CASAs or by the State Court Administrative Office for attorneys.

Author's note: Determining the objectives of the child advocacy is often not a problem. The advocate wants to see the child protected and, during a period of family rehabilitation, wants to see some consistency in the child's daily life so that it is disrupted as little as possible. A child's sense of time needs to be respected and decisions made in a timely manner. Current law requires the advocate to represent the best interests of the child, but that high-sounding phrase is amiguous and subjective. A perennial question in child advocacy has been, "What voice ought the child to have in identifying his or her best interests and the goals of the advocacy?"

In this proposal, the child advocate is charged with representing the best interests of the child if the child is under fourteen. Over age fourteen, however, this proposal creates a rebuttable presumption that a CASA must seek and represent to the probate court a child's wishes. This age coincides with that at which a child can consent to adoption in many states or request removal of a testamentary guardian. This proposal draws a line age fourteen, saying that at that age the youngster, with guidance from the advocate and others, should have the right to a voice before the court. The judge need not accept the position put forth by the advocate in each case, but at least the child's voice is presented and heard. In a rare case the court may choose to appoint a guardian ad litem to represent the best interests of a child,—particularly where the youngster is under a further disability. This proposal is also consistent with the Model Rules of Professional Conduct, which provide that laywers, as far as reasonably possible, maintain a normal lawyer-client relationship with a minor client (Model Rules of Professional Conduct 1.14).

Some have argued that age fourteen is too high, that children as young as seven or eight may have the capacity and should have the right to direct their representatives. See, e.g., Ramsey, "Representation of the Child in Protection Proceedings: The Determination of Decision-making Capacity," Family Law

Quarterly, 17 (1983): 287. Others have argued that the weight given to the youngster's voice should be left to a case-by-case determination so that the advocate could always overrule the youngster on what is in his or her best interests. These proposals have their own limitations. We propose that the child's wishes always be considered by the advocate in determining the child's best interests but that they be determinative after age fourteen unless the youngster is under a serious mental or emotional disability. Of course, the advocate should counsel and advise the child as the youngster is trying to decide what his or her goals are.

VIII. Confidentiality, Immunity, and Notice

A. All records and information acquired or reviewed by a CASA and all reports prepared by the CASA are confidential and shall be disclosed only pursuant to court rules or other state and federal law.

B. The state and local boards, state and local directors, coordinators, staff and volunteer attorneys, and CASAs participating in the CASA program shall not be civilly liable for acts or omissions committed in connection with the duties that are part of the program if they have acted in good faith and are not guilty of gross negligence.

C. The CASA shall be considered a party to the child protection proceedings and be notified of all court hearings as provided by court rule.

Appendix B: Checklist of Ten Dimensions of Child Advocacy

1. Investigation and Fact Finding

- [ ] What harm has the child suffered? What happened? where? when? how? by whom? How serious is the harm suffered? Does the child remain at risk? What are the options for protecting the child from further harm?
- [ ] What is the family composition?
- [ ] What is the family's immediate home environment like?
- [ ] What are the parents like? What are their strengths? weaknesses? personal history of abuse or neglect? substance abuse or psychiatric problems?
- [ ] What is the child like? Is his or her social-psychological development normal for his or her age? How does the child do in school? Does he or she have special needs?
- [ ] Has the child contributed to the abuse or neglect? If so, how?

At Review and Permanency Planning Hearings:

- [ ] Using the case plan as a checklist, the advocate should inquire as to significant new developments since the dispositional hearing.
- [ ] What progress has been made toward alleviating the conditions that caused the child to be placed in foster care or that cause the child to remain in foster care?
- [ ] If the child is placed with the parents, what progress has been made toward alleviating the conditions that cause him or her to remain under court supervision?

2. Consultation

☐ What do the social worker, and other professionals involved in the case think the major problems are? What do they think should happen?

☐ What do the parents and other family members think the major problems are? What do they think should happen?

☐ What do the advocate's supervising professionals think the major problems are? What do they think should happen?

3. Assessment

☐ Does the court have sufficient information and professional advice about the child, the family, and the presenting problems?

☐ What other assessment or professional evaluation is needed?

☐ Who will do what, when?

4. Identifying the Child's Interests

☐ Is the child protected from physical and emotional harm?

☐ Is the child provided adequate food, clothing, shelter, guidance, and supervision?

☐ Have all reasonable efforts been made to protect the child in his home?

☐ If the child is placed, does the placement disrupt the child's life as little as possible?

☐ Is the placement in the least restrictive (most family-like setting)?

☐ Are regular and frequent visits with the parent(s) arranged?

☐ Is the case proceeding in a timely manner?

☐ Are necessary services being promptly provided to the child and family?

5. Permanency Planning

☐ Is the child's home safe, or can it be made safe pending further proceedings?

☐ What reasonable efforts can be made to prevent or eliminate the need for out-of-home placement?

☐ Is the normal pattern of the child's life disrupted as little as possible?

☐ How long is the placement likely to continue? Is the current placement available for as long as the child might need to be in placement?

☐ Has frequent visitation been arranged, or is there compelling reason not to allow visits between parent and child?

☐ Is adequate progress being made toward permanency for the child?

6. Client Counseling

☐ Does the child have questions about the court process?

☐ How does the child feel about options presented by all parties to this point?

☐ What does the child want to see happen as a result of these proceedings?

☐ Where does the child want to live now?

☐ What other preferences does the child have about placement, visitation, school and so forth?

☐ What does the child want communicated to the court, social worker, or parent(s)?

7. Decision Making and Coming to a Tentative Position

☐ What should the advocate be prepared to recommend to the court?

☐ Where should the child be placed? Should the advocate recommend that the child be returned home?

☐ What visitation should be arranged or ordered?

☐ Are additional medical or psychological exams necessary?

☐ What additional services does the advocate think are necessary to rectify the conditions that caused the child to be placed in foster care or to remain in foster care?

☐ What additional actions does the advocate think need to be taken by the parent or guardian, to correct the conditions that caused the child to be placed in foster care or to remain in foster care?

☐ Should the advocate recommend steps be taken toward termination of parental rights or some other permanent plan away from the natural parents?

☐ What other matters can be dealt with at this hearing?

☐ What are the goals of the advocate at this time?

8. Problem Solving and Mediation

☐ What are the common interests among the parties?

☐ Can the advocate promote a cooperative resolution of any of the problems?

☐ Can any other institutions besides child welfare and the courts assist in addressing any problems?

9. Identifying Action Steps

☐ What needs to be done to protect the child?

☐ What action does the advocate want the court to take?

☐ What action should the social worker take?

☐ What action should others take?

☐ Who is to do what, when? What services does the family need? How will these services be provided? by whom? when?

10. Follow-up

☐ Identify steps to be taken by advocate and others before the next court appearance.

☐ Contact principals either in person or by telephone to get the steps accomplished.

☐ Keep a tickler system of reminders of important follow-up steps.

Index

About the Author

Donald N. Duquette is clinical professor of law and director of the Child Advocacy Law Clinic at the University of Michigan Law School. He writes and teaches extensively on interdisciplinary approaches to child welfare issues. His research on the role of the representative of the child in protection cases (conducted with Sarah H. Ramsey) earned the Research in Advocacy Award from the National Association of Court Appointed Special Advocates in 1985.